EVOLUTION OF LIFE AND FORM

EVOLUTION OF LIFE AND FORM

Four Lectures Delivered at the Twenty-Third Anniversary Meeting of the Theosophical Society at Adyar, Madras, 1898

BY

ANNIE BESANT

GYAN

ISBN: 978-81-212-1886-3 (HB)
First Published, 1899
Published, 2018
Published by

Gyan Publishing House
5, Ansari Road
Daryaganj, New Delhi-110002
Phone: 011-47034999, 9811692060
www.gyanbooks.com
E-mail: books@gyanbooks.com

Printed at: G. Print Process, Delhi.

CONTENTS.

[FIRST LECTURE.]

ANCIENT AND MODERN SCIENCE.

MY BROTHERS:—The subject on which I am to address you this morning, and the three mornings that follow, is one of considerable complexity and difficulty. I do not apologise to you for the difficulty of my theme. When we meet here in our Anniversary Meeting, we meet as students and not simply as superficial men and women of the world. We try to prepare ourselves, by study, for the exchange of thought which in these gatherings takes place, and although the subject is a difficult one, although it is not possible to make it clear and intelligible without the use of certain technical terms, yet, to the student technical terms—being precise—are really the easiest to understand, and inasmuch as, in a great majority at least, we are students, I who speak, and you who listen, we may be content to treat the subject in a somewhat formal and technical way. Roughly, my outline is this. I want to lay before you an intelligible conception of evolution, taking it on its two sides, that of the evolving life and that of the developing forms. I begin by laying before you a sketch of the methods of "Ancient and Modern Science," the direction in which each has worked, and is working, the ultimate union that, we hope, may take place between them. For what could more fully presage the good of the whole world, what could promise more happily for the relationship between the different races of humanity, than to draw together on the plane of mind the science of antiquity and of modern days, the science of the East and of the West, and, by wedding them to each other, draw together the nations that are now divided, and make objective that brotherhood of humanity of which we dream.

Dealing first with ancient and modern science in this broad and general way, and taking that as my subject for this morning, I shall pass on to-morrow to speak on the "Functions of the Gods," meaning by that phrase the activities of that invisible side of nature on which the whole of the visible depends. Whether we use here the name "Devas" to represent those developed spiritual intelligences, or whether with the child of Islâm, with the Hebrew or the Christian, we speak of the "Angels" and "Archangels," the name matters nothing; the conception is common to every faith of man. We shall study their functions in the universe, and try to understand how they act as the ministers of the Divine Will. Then we shall pass on to treat of that "Evolution of Life" which lies underneath the evolution of forms. Finally, we shall treat the "Evolution of Forms," and see how, in that evolution, is the promise of final perfection, how all is working to a perfect ending, how the best that we can dream of is less than the performance of God.

That is the outline of our work. Let us at once begin the first section of the subject—Ancient and Modern Science.

Now, in the olden times, in those times to which in this land our thought turns back most fondly with reverence and with pride, in those times, here, as in every other ancient land, Religion and Science were wedded together, and there was no discord between the intelligence and the spirit. It matters not whither you wander amid the ancient nations of the world: you may travel through the whole of Chaldea; you may study the remains of ancient Egypt; you may go through Persia and search amid her monuments; you may cross the Atlantic to America, and unbury the cities that were lost ere yet the Aztecs had made the mighty State which fell under the blows of the Spaniards; you may go into China and, in the vast recesses of that well-nigh unknown land, you may search for what has been left there from ancient days; or without going outside the limits of your own land, you may take the literature that is our pride, the mighty books written by the Rishis of the past; and everywhere antiquity speaks with a single tongue. Religion reveals the spirit, the spiritual truth which is one. Intelligence studies that truth in its manifold manifestations, and its work; science, studying the phenomena which are images of aspects of the Divine, is the handmaid, is the sister, of religion, and between them discord is unnatural and fatal to progress. That is the ancient view; but when we come to our own century a new phenomenon presents itself to our gaze—religion on the one side suspicious of science in its progress, science on the other hand apt to be proudly contemptuous of religious claims. How has the divorce arisen? Why this discord between two of the great helpers of human evolution? The reason is not far to seek. In the western world the science of the elder time, the science of antiquity, disappeared in the great flood of barbaric invasions, underneath the whirlpool caused by the ruins of the Roman Empire, and later on, underneath the wreckage of that same Empire with its new centre in Constantinople. The invasions of barbarians, both from the East and the North, sweeping over the European continent, brought ignorance in the wake of barbaric conquest. The result was that night came down upon knowledge and thick darkness enveloped the lands which were to be the nursery of a new civilisation. When the Sun of science again began to rise upon the Western world, it presented itself in a form which was alien, nay, which was more than alien, which was hostile to the dominant religion of the time. It came from the children of Islâm. It came from those who recognised Muhammed as their Prophet. From the Muslim schools of Arabia came the first teachers of modern science to Europe. True, they were really by their intellectual ancestry descended from the thought of Greece. They drew their inspiration from the school of Plato through the Neo-Platonists; they reproduced the ideas of Porphyry and Ptolemy, and of other Grecian and Egyptian thinkers, Neo-Platonic and even Gnostic. But they threw over it the garb of Islâm, they presented it in the form of Arabic thought. The result of this was that, as it made its way into Spain in the wake of the conquering Moors, as it came with those who drove out of the Southern Peninsula the rule of the Spanish Christian monarchy, so the first aspect of science to Christians was an aspect of hostility. It came as an invading enemy and not as an illuminant to all. Hence conflict arose; some who were within the limits of the mighty Church of Rome, touched by a longing for the new learning, stretched out their hands to take the gifts that science was bringing. These men were regarded with suspicion nay, with more than suspicion, with hatred that broke out in bitter persecution. Who can read the history of Roger Bacon, the wondrous monk; who can picture Copernicus on his death-bed as his immortal work is brought to him ere yet his eyes are closed, he having shrunk from earlier publication, lest the stake should be his portion; who can stand in the Field of Flowers in Rome, and see there the statue erected where he was burned to death, who dying in one century, lives for all centuries to come—Giordano Bruno; who can listen to Galileo, as with faltering lips he denies the truth he knows and utters the falsehood that he knows not; who can follow these martyr-steps, led on by bitter memories of blood and fire, without understanding the reason for the hostility of science to religion, without confessing with shame and sorrow that that hostility was caused and was justified by the cruelties wreaked by religion on science, when science was young and feeble? Every one of us who stands upon the side of religion should recognise that we are reaping the bitter harvest of our own past errors, and that the law is just which brings upon us the difficult and opposition we encounter in our modern da For as science grew strong, she grew strong wi the sword in her hands. She fought for every in of the ground on which she stood, and only so as she could guard herself was she safe from t flame or from the prison. Hence she searched everything in nature that could serve as a weap against the foe that attacked her. Hence s welcomed eagerly everything which seemed show that materialism was the true philosophy life. If we go back twenty-five years, to the ti when I and some of you were young, we shall fi that over western science there hung the shad of materialism, and that stronger and strong grew the scientific tendency to "see in matter t promise and the potency of every form of lif You remember those famous words of Profes Tyndall, no materialist in his thought and religious man in his aspirations, but wellni driven by despair to claim fair field for scien and to fling back the claims of religion, beca among them was included the right to gag, t refusal to allow thought to be honestly utte by the thinker. But things are changing m and more; as religion has been growing m liberal and more rational, science is becoming l materialistic and less aggressive; and we shall see presently that the most modern of modern science—not quite the science that you get in your text-books, for that is practically out-of-date in the rush of thought which comes from the West, but the science of the leaders of thought, the science of the first men in the scientific camp—is more and more approaching the domain where scientists will recognise religion as helper and not as enemy. In fact, speaking from the same chair from which Tyndall had uttered his famous phrase that "in matter he saw the promise and potency of every form of life," his successor, Sir William Crookes, a member of our own Theosophical Society, declared, reversing those words of his predecessor, that "In life I see the promise and potency of all forms of matter."

Such is the great change. Let us now examine in detail. The fundamental difference between ancient and modern science is that ancient science studies the world from the standpoint of life which is evolving, while modern science studies the world by observing the forms through which that life is manifesting. The first studies life, and sees in forms the expressions of life. The second studies forms, and tries, by the process of induction, to find out if there be an underlying principle by which the multiplicity of forms may be explained. The first works from above downwards, the second from below upwards, and in that very fact is the promise of a meeting place where the two will join hand in hand. But this fundamental difference carries with it very important results. If we are to study the world from the standpoint of forms, our study will be almost endless in its multiplicity. Think of a tree; the one trunk through which the life is pouring, innumerable leaves in which that life is ultimately expressed; it is an image of the tree of life, that great Ashvattha, the tree of which we have heard, whose roots are in the heavens and whose branches spread out over the earth. If we are to study it where its trunk is, the trunk of life, we have the unity of purpose and can trace why we have multiplicity of forms; but if we are to start at the parts where the leaves are growing, leaf by leaf we must examine, every difference of outline we must record, each little variety in shape we must carefully note and study. Science studies the leaves in modern days—the old science studied the life. There is the fundamental difference. There is also the reason of the difference of methods by which the study must be carried on. What is the method of modern science? The use of clear observation, keen judgment, power of placing like things together, and seeing the differences that divide the classes of the like from the classes of the unlike. But in order that this may be done, inasmuch as nature is infinite both in the vast and in the minute, man demands, to supplement his limited senses, instruments and apparatus of the most exquisite and delicate character; so that it has been even said that the progress of science is the progress of the exquisite nature of the apparatus which science uses, and scientific men will devise a more delicate balance, a more dainty way of adjustment, instrument after instrument, until perfection seems well-nigh to be reached; the modern man of science, to carry on his researches, demands a vast array of apparatus that he must use for his work, for according to the delicacy of his apparatus is the extent of his observation of the forms to which his attention is directed. But the man of science of the ancient type does not ask for instruments; he is not studying the evolution of forms; he has to study life, not form; and for such study he must evolve himself, the life that is within him, for only life can measure life, only life can respond to the vibrations of the living; his work is to unfold himself, to bring out of the depths of his own nature the divine powers that lie hidden therein, not in the senses but in the Self. His investigations can only be carried on by means of these powers, and only as he develops the divine within him will he be able to understand and measure the divine without him. Now this is only possible because, in essence, the natures of God and man are identical. This sounds a bold statement, but it is the fundamental truth of all religions. Need I quote to you the famous saying, "Thou art That"? Shall I take an equivalent phrase from the Hebrew Scripture, accepted by the whole Christian world: "God created man in His own image, in the image of God created He him"? The teaching is identical as all great truths are identical in the various religions; but what does it mean? God is manifest in His universe. Would you understand His work, you must develop the God within yourself, else will He for ever be veiled from your eyes. Not by the eyes of sense may you behold Him, not by the vision of intellect may you see that Form, invisible even to the intelligence. Only as the Self that is God is unfolded within you, will the Self that is the God without you manifest to you the full glory of His life. That is the ancient starting point. Thus what the man of old had to do, if indeed he were to be a man of science, was to become divine; he was to be a saint before he could be a sage. No man could be wise until he was pure, for how should impure eyes behold the Pure? There : the hall-mark of the man of science of the ancier days: he is developed within before he can be learne without. But from the modern man of scienc is not demanded this condition. He must indee lead a life that is self-restrained, orderly, and fairl clean; were he to yield to the riot of the senses, h: intelligence would become clouded. He must hav keen power of observation, balanced strength (judgment, strong patience, unwearied industry, cleа insight for differences and similarities. All thes are demanded from him, if he is to be great, an these are among the noblest powers of intelligenc But all he asks of religion is to leave him alone. C old, religion opened the gateway to science; now a-days science asks nothing from religion save t stand aside. That is the difficulty in our way. W have to show that life cannot be understood unt the student lives that which he seeks. That even th understanding of forms is very imperfect until th life expressed through them is recognised an partially understood. That fundamental differenc of method then, will cover the whole field, and wi enable us to comprehend the difference of the result:

Now let us try to understand more clearly why i was that the ancient man of science was taught tha the first step to true knowledge, or wisdom, was th unfolding of the Self. What is life or consciousness—for the two terms are synonymous? It is the power to answer to vibrations, the power to respond—that is consciousness. Evolution is the unfolding of a continually increasing power to respond. The whole universe is full of the vibrations of Íshvara, of God. He sustains and moves the whole. Consciousness is the power in us to answer to those vibrations. All powers lie hidden within us as the oak tree lies hidden in the acorn. But it is in the process of evolution that the sapling slowly grows out of the seed. In Eternity, in the Now, all is existent, perfect; in Time only is there succession, the unfolding of one thing after another. In the changeless Point everything is present: Space is but the field for diverse sequences. Hence Time and Space are the basic illusions, and are yet the fundamental conditions of thinking. Keep, I pray you, that definition of consciousness in mind, for it will govern the remainder of our study.

The Self in man, being in the image of God, is triple as the Self, the Divine, is triple. I need not stop to argue this. You know it from that great literature which lies at the foundation of all Hindu Philosophy. Whether you speak in abstract terms and say with the Upanishad that Brahman is threefold, whether you speak of Him as Sat-chit-ânanda, or whether, instead of using philosophical, abstrac terms, you say He is manifest as Íshvara in th Trimûrti as Mahâdeva, Vishnu and Brahmâ, i matters not. You may take the concrete form o the abstract, the fundamental idea is the same: tha the Divine Self in manifestation is triple, and there fore in every great religion God is spoken of as a Trinity. If this were not so, the relationshi between God and man would remain for ever un intelligible, for man shows a triplicity as he evolves The human reflection of that triple Divine Self i the triple Self in man.

One by one are the Divine aspects unfolded a manifestation proceeds. The lowest, if I may dar to use such a term, is the aspect which is firs brought into activity for the building of the univers So also in man the intelligence awakens and become active, the lowest aspect of the human Self. Tha is the reflection of Brahmâ, of the Universal Mind the creative energy from which all comes forth and you may find in yourselves, as you evolve, tha creative faculty of imagination which, working a present in subtle matter, will, when man is per fect, work in grosser matter as well; for th imaginative power in man is the reflection of th power that in God created the universe. Brahm meditated, and all forms came forth; and in th creative power of mind lies every possibility of form. So in man is later evolved the next aspect, that of A'nanda, where unity is recognised instead of diversity. Chit, in man, is the intelligence that *knows*, that separates and divides and analyses, and it has to do with the multiplicity of forms and with their inter-relations; A'nanda is the wisdom that realises the unity of all things, and that accomplishes union, thus finding the joy that lies at the very heart of life; last of all in human evolution, is developed the third and highest aspect of Deity, Self-Existence, the Unity that lies beyond union, and this can be developed in man only because man is one with the Eternal in his nature. By this evolution, in ages to come, through the countless kalpas that lie in front, Íshvara after Íshvara arises, each as the fruitage of a universe, to carry on still more mightily the will of the "One without a second," and to manifest something of that perfection to the whole of the then manifested nature. Such, very roughly, is the course of human evolution into divinity, and this is carried on by races succeeding one another; as we come to the higher Root-races of man, to those that we speak of as the Fifth, in which we are, the Sixth, that shall succeed us, and the Seventh that finishes this cycle of human evolution, we learn that the characteristic of each of these three Root-races is that each gradually develops that aspect of God which belongs to it in the due sequence of evolution. The Fifth is developing the aspect of Chit, Intelligence, the mind is being evolved, and all the progress of modern science, so marked in our own days, is but part of the fruitage of that evolution, of that growth of intelligence which looks on the outer world as not itself—as the Not-Self—and seeks to study and understand it. The characteristic attributes belonging to the evolution of the two following races are even now to be reached by special methods, by individuals who are willing to take the pains to make the required sacrifices. That which we know as Yoga is the method by which evolution is quickened in the individual, and all the powers of the Self, up to the threshold of divinity, may by it be brought into manifestation in the man of the present. That is why Yoga training was necessary for the ancient scientist; he must develop in himself the three aspects of God, if he were to understand them as manifested in the universe around him.

Now, at our own stage of evolution, it is specially the life of Brahmâ—or the Brahmâ aspect of God—with which the human mind is coming into touch, because the mind in man is the reflection of the universal mind in Kosmos. That life is the life that is the force in the atom, that vivifies every atom, nay, that brings the atom into existence, as we shall see, and remains during the whole of the growth of the universe as the fundamental life that keeps those atoms as active particles building up innumerable forms. Only as the life of Brahmâ, the aspect of Brahmâ, is developed in the human Self will man be able to study the workings of that life in the atomic forms that are filled by it; and it is very significant that some of the greatest problems of modern science are now turning on the nature of the atom, and that scientists are asking, what is it? Is it matter or force? Is it a particle or a vortex? Never will that question be answered with certainty until man has developed in himself the power to respond to the life that thrills in the atom, until, developing intelligence within himself to the fullest point, he is able to answer by that intelligence to the vibrations of the atomic life outside him. We have defined consciousness as the power to answer to vibrations, and if man is to measure life, if he is to know the underlying causes of phenomena, he must develop in himself the power to respond to that life outside him; and in the perfection of human intelligence—the reflection of the Brahmâ aspect of God—lies the only possibility of solution for this much debated problem in science. I said it was significant, for this problem belongs to the Fifth race, and th Western world is at present peopled largely by th fifth sub-race of the great Fifth. Thus it takes t the very highest point the concrete mind of mar that marvellous activity of the intellect, that swi and yet patient study, bringing about the achieve ments that modern science is performing. A these are a testimony of the truth of the ancier teaching that sub-race after sub-race arises, each on with its own work to do, and we should look o the work of each sub-division of humanity as goo in itself: each should not be regarded as a isolated and hostile expression, but as part of th Divine manifestation, expressing that portio which it is destined to express.

Looking thus, then, on the problem of the life tha exists in the atom, we find that in order to under stand it, we must develop the pure intellect in man but to understand the life that clothes itself i organic forms, to unravel the secrets which wil explain to us why one is formed thus and anothe thus, the next great aspect of the Self must b developed within us—that of the all-pervading lif of Vishnu, that sustains the world as the might supporter of everything, the basis, the foundation o the whole. There alone is unifying energy an there the root from which all divisions have arisen only as we realise this aspect of unifying energy in the Self will the secrets of organised forms in nature unravel themselves before our eyes. This work is that of the Sixth Root-race, and those who would ante-date their evolution must develop Sixth-race powers in themselves by Yoga. Remains one mightier problem, subtlest and most difficult of all, that of the life of the human spirit, of man evolving into God. The mysteries of that life may only be understood when the human Self, which comes forth from the Father of all—from the mighty One who is sometimes the Destroyer, sometimes the Creator, but always the Regenerator, the name that includes them both, Mahâdeva, the mighty God who is Sat, Existence—has developed the aspect of Sat, of pure Existence, thus becoming the triple Unity, a Logos, an Íshvara. That is the work of the Seventh Root-race, and when that is accomplished, then only will the final problems of the human spirit lie open before our gaze.

The scientific man of antiquity, then, began by that self-attention, unfolding in himself one by one all those potentialities under a suitable Guru, passing from step to step till he reached the highest, and ever worshipping the Mahâguru, the Guru of the universe. Having unfolded his highest powers, he began to study life, life in its outpouring, not life in its manifold and veiled manifestations in the lower worlds. Hence the lofty point at which he started, no less than the arising of Íshvara enveloped in Mâyâ.

What is Íshvara? What is Mâyâ? There is the first great problem. Let us reverently address ourselves to it. The philosophers of India have answered these questions in different ways, each one containing part of the eternal truth. Íshvara is that mighty centre of consciousness that exists unchanged in the bosom of the One Existence. There are innumerable such Centres of Consciousness, of which you may remember your own Svâmi Subba Rao wrote as existing in the bosom of the One Existence. Íshvara in manifestation is like a lamp, a light enclosed in a shade. Íshvara, enveloped in Mâyâ, brings forth a universe and is enclosed, as it were, in the universe of which He is the Light. Breaking the shade, the light shines forth in every direction. Dissolving the universe, He still remains. The centre remains, but the circumference that circumscribed it is gone. So is that mighty centre when the universe vanishes; He alone remains, holding His centre unshaken in the very act of merging in, expanding into, the Infinite, the Absolute, the Super-Consciousness, the One. Let us think of Him as an eternal centre of self-consciousness, able to merge in super-consciousness and to again limit Himself to self-consciousness.

What, then, is Mâyâ? Mâyâ is prepared in every case by the merging in Íshvara of the whole of the universe which is come to its ending. As one loka rolls up and merges in the one above it, all forms in the loka thus merged disappear, but the consciousness that ensouled those forms does not vanish; a modification of consciousness remains, a modification expressing itself by a vibratory power—not a vibration, but a power to vibrate in a particular way; and though the form vanishes as the loka is merged in the one above it—because the matter disappears, being disintegrated into finer matter—in consciousness there remains the power to vibrate in the way in which it had vibrated in the grosser matter, and power persists although the forms caused by such vibrations disappear, for lack of material sufficiently coarse to respond to such vibrations. As one region passes into the next, this process is repeated over and over and over again, and loka after loka vanishes. The forms are gone, the vibrations are gone, only the modifications in consciousness capable of giving rise to similar vibrations remain until finally, when Íshvara—whose consciousness was the one consciousness in the universe, whose life was the one life, who supported every form, who made the possibility of every separated existence—gathers up His universe into Himself ere He merges Himself in the ONE, everything has vanished that we know as form, nothing remains save the centre of consciousness. There remains in Íshvara the power of vibrating in particular fashions, resulting from the evolution of His universe, in endless multiplicity of vibrations; when He merges Himself in the One Existence all has vanished as form, but powers remain in these subtle modifications, preserved in that unchangeable centre in the mightiness of the One Life. Is that only a dream?

There was a great teacher, Vâsiṣhtha. He taught Râmâ, as you will remember, and in the record of his teaching there are hints on some of the mysteries of life. If you keep what I have now said in mind, if I have succeeded by the clumsy words which are all that the human tongue can utter on these great problems, in clarifying at all your thoughts, then just listen to that same thought as expressed by Sûryadeva, when he was speaking of the same thing—the ending and the new beginning of a universe. We have only to add to what I have already said, that when Íshvara arises in order that a new universe may be formed, He throws His life into these modifications that had apparently disappeared, and the Mâyâ in which He arises, enveloped and circumscribed, is His own re-vivified memory, which can never be separated from Himself; He draws in His consciousness, under the impulse of the Great Breath, limiting it to self-consciousness, and turning His attention to the contents of that self-consciousness, its powers start into activity, and that is Mâyâ. So it is written: "Thereafter, Thou, O Lord, intent on [maintaining] the reign of night, fixed within the Self, having indrawn that order of things, [or universe.] . . . . . . To-day, Thou hast awakened, and art most joyfully desirous of again throwing out [manifesting] the universe in mighty gradations [hierachies of beings]." [*Yoga Vâsiṣhtha*, lxxxvii, 7, 8.] These nights and days are the "Nights and Days of Brahmâ," the inbreathing and outbreathing of the One Existence, and Mâyâ is this indrawn "order of things" that remains fixed through the Night, and starts forth as Íshvara awakens at the coming of Day. That is Mâyâ; and if you take up the definitions given in the different schools, you will find that this includes and illumines every one of them, that it shows you what is meant by illusion, and explains to you what is implied in dreaming. The joyful throwing out into manifestation of all the powers that are remembered by Íshvara the moment His attention is turned to His own Self, that memory-prompted "desire" which arises in the bosom of the Eternal, is the root of the coming universe. Now this thought will prove to you the key of much ancient teaching. You have, in the Universal Mind full of ideas which are not yet concreted into phenomena, the world of ideas of Plato, the invisible world of the Hebrew Kabbalah; in every great teaching you find the same thought expressed. If, instead of being fettered by words, as for the most part we are, and if, instead of repeating phrases that carry with them no idea in the mind of the repeater, we would try to read the thought that underlies the words, we should find the Hindu philosphy in every modern philosophy that is worthy of the name, and see the traces of ancient India in Greece and in Rome, in Germany and in the England of to-day.

What is the next stage? The Life-Breath goes forth. Íshvara, the Centre of all, enveloped in Mâyâ sends forth His breath; as that vibrating breath falls on the enveloping Mâyâ, Mâyâ becomes Prakriti, or Matter—rather, perhaps, Mûlaprakriti, the root of matter. As that breath, with its triple vibratory force falls on this matter, it throws it into three modifications, or "attributes"—Tamas, inertia, or better, stability; Rajas, activity, vigour; Sattva, a difficult word to translate: I am inclined to translate it as Harmony; for this reason, that wherever there is pleasure, Sattva is present. Without harmony no pleasure can anywhere exist. All pleasure is due to harmonious vibration, and that quality of harmonious inter-related vibrations is the quality that Sattva gives to matter. These three fundamental qualities of matter—answering to three fundamental modifications in the consciousness of Íshvara—inertia, activity, and harmony, these are the famous three Gunas without which Prakriti cannot manifest. Fundamental, essential, and unchangeable, they are present in every particle in the manifested universe, and according to their combinations is the nature of each particle.

Then comes the seven-fold division. In a moment I will tell you why we speak of it as seven-fold instead of five-fold, which is the more familiar division to you. The seven-fold division, what is this? Here is matter with its three Gunas, now ready to receive another impulse from the Life-Breath; that breath comes forth from Brahmâ, for Íshvara has unfolded His triple nature into its three aspects, and it comes forth in seven great waves. Each one modifies matter, and evolves and ensouls those that follow it. The first two are absolutely beyond our knowing, and belong not to our present stages of evolution at all; therefore they are ordinarily left out, and only the five that make up the evolution of our universe are spoken of in the sacred books. Here and there the seven are mentioned, but only rarely. You may remember the seven tongues of fire, for instance, and one or two other similar phrases. But generally five-fold is Prâna, the five-fold evolving life. First, in every case, is a modification of consciousness sent forth as a power by Íshvara. Turn to the *Vishnu Purâna* and you will see exactly the stage that I am pointing out to you in more modern phrases. Íshvara Himself, as Brahmâ, sends forth a power, due to a modification of His consciousness, called in the *Vishnu Purâna* a Tanmâtra. In the English translation the word rudiment is used. You remember the rudiments of sound, of touch, of colour, and so on. All these rudiments are the tanmâtras. These tanmâtras are the powers due to modifications in consciousness or life, without which no modification in matter can be. The consciousness first, then the form. The first great vibration that goes forth is the vibration that gives rise to what we speak of here as sound—all our terms being drawn from the lowest, or physical, manifestations; the form that it brings into manifestation is A'kâsha, the mighty element of Ether; not the ether of modern science, of course, although that is its physical representative. Then into that the next tanmâtra, the next power due to a modification of consciousness, is sent forth; the A'kâsha, with the primary vibration within it, receives the second vibration sent out by Íshvara, and this, pervading the matter around it, brings about the next modification of matter, the element Vâyu, or Air. Vâyu, permeated, ensouled and enveloped in A'kâsha, receives a fresh impulse from Íshvara, the third tanmâtra, or power resulting from a modification of consciousness; this tanmâtra, working on Vâyu, produces the modification of matter called the element Agni, or Fire, and this fire-matter is permeated, ensouled, and enveloped in Vâyu, as Vâyu in A'kâsha. A similar process brings into manifestation the elements Apas and Prithivî. The "magnetic field" of an atom is composed of all the tanmâtras and elements above it. Try to realise this process if you can, though I know the conception is difficult. What has occurred? A modification of life or consciousness in Íshvara, manifested as a power, a vibration; everything depends on vibration; ancient and modern science speak alike on this. The universe is made up of vibrations, the vibrations which are the modifications of the Divine outpouring of life. These clothe themselves in fundamental forms of matter, out of which all multiplicity is developed. These modifications in matter, these great, or primary, elements are also called tattvas. Tanmâtras, then, are the powers sent out by modifications of consciousness, and these are awkwardly translated by the word rudiments; we have next the modifications in matter, the great elements, the primary elements, or tattvas. The first of the tattvas is called A'kâsha; then Vâyu, then Agni, then Apas, then Prithivî, the five following one after the other; the keynote of this evolution is that the modification of the previous higher tattva is reproduced within the lower, pervades it and expands outside it. If you will take the *Vishnu Purâna*, the second chapter, and read over again the evolution of the five tattvas, you will find that the Sanskrit word which is used comes from a root which means to pervade as well as to enclose, giving the idea of permeation as well as of expanding around to form an envelope. And you must understand that the central life of each tattva is the preceding tattva with its tanmâtra; that, with the new tanmâtra, makes up the life; and the outer form is the new tattva that by that productive action comes into existence.

Now leaving that, for I cannot go into further details, let me just say to you one word about the seven and the five, because that has been a source of great dispute between some of our Hindu Pandits and some of our Theosophists. In the universe, taken as a whole, seven-fold is the life of Íshvara. Beyond the tattva that we know as A'kâsha, there is that tattva which has been called Anupâdaka, and beyond that A'ditattva, the first. Those are far beyond our knowing; we cannot think so far. For our life-evolution, the five mark the limit; and only the five, therefore, as a rule, are given in the books which are to be studied to show you how to evolve.

Rapidly we must pass onward, then, to these tattvas as, modifying themselves by aggregations, and by disintegrations and re-combinations of these, they make innumerable forms. The fundamental conception is that there are as many basic forms of atoms in the universe as there are tattvas. The tattva of ancient science is the atom of modern science, but modern science makes the mistake of supposing that there is only one fundamental atom. The truth is that modern science is only seeking to get hold of the Prithivî Tattva, the lowest, or physical, atom, and it has not yet recognized even the existence of the four (or six) higher atoms that stretch beyond. These atoms form the regions of the universe. All that is physical is made up from the Prithivî Tattva. Not only is this so, but within the limits of this physical region, correspondences of all the higher six atomic forms are reproduced. The sub-divisions of the physical region, due to combinations of the Prithivî Tattva, show forth the characteristics of the great regions which make up the universe; so that we have here in our solid, liquid, gas, three ethers and atoms, correspondences of the six higher tattvas, but we have them all in their Prithivî form; they are the modifications of Prithivî, reproducing on a lower plane the great primary elements. We might call them Prithivî A'ditattva, Prithivî Anupâdhakatattva, Prithivî A'kâshatattva, Prithivî Vâyutattva, Prithivî Agnitattva, Prithivî Apastattva, Prithivî Prithivîtattva. Above the region of Prithivî comes the great realm of Apas, with similar sub-divisions, all of the Apastattva, and so again another seven above that in the higher realm of Agni, and above that the same in the still higher realm of Vâyu, and above that again in the A'kâsha and then the highest two unknown realms. When you remember that all these regions interpenetrate the one the other, you will gain some glimpse of a complexity dizzying to think of, the vast complexity of the universe in which the One Life is working. Yet that complexity is simplified by thus working downwards, and there is the line of the study of the ancient science. Working out from this originally simple life into the endless multiplicity of forms, we may trace the One among the many, and see the Self in all things, and all things in Him.

At the ending of a universe, the tattvas merge in each other by disintegration; Prithivî Tattva, having disintegrated into atoms, these atoms are themselves broken up, and the tanmâtra that formed them, being no longer able to express itself for lack of suitable material, ceases to be a power, and remains only represented by a modification in consciousness—a permanent possibility. Thus Apas Tattva becomes the lowest manifestation, and, by a repetition of the above process, ceases to exist. In like fashion each successively vanishes. Hence, Mahâdeva is represented as saying in the *Shivâgama:* "The universe proceeded from the tattvas; it goes on through the tattvas; it vanishes into the tattvas."

Such is the grandiose conception of the kosmos given by the science of antiquity; one life, pulsing into innumerable vibrations, and these throwing matter into forms. On this was based the Pythagorean system of numbers; on this mathematics and music were founded; on this the "Great Science," or Magic, of long-perished nations was built up. That science only survives in its purity in the Great White Brotherhood, but its traces may yet be seen in the scriptures and the religions of the world.

We take up modern science, and pass into a different atmosphere. Now phenomena are to be studied, forms are to occupy our attention. But as we look at modern science we find that it is beginning to transcend the study of forms; we find the efforts of its greatest men are turned to seek unity amid diversity. Do not think that, in speaking of modern science as studying forms, I am indifferent to the mighty achievements that it has made, or that I would say one word in derogation of the ability of the leading men of science, and the priceless value of the work that they are doing for humanity. Their achievements during the present century are achievements that are worthy of the very deepest respect, not only for the "sublime patience of the investigator," of which William Kingdon Clifford so rightly spoke, but also for the self-abnegation with which many of them have given their lives to follow truth, to study in the innermost recesses of the phenomena of nature what secrets she has hidden, what may be underneath the "Veil of Isis." I do not, then, speak a word against modern science, but I point out to you this fact, that the greatest work of science has been the generalisations that have been suggested in the attempt to reach simplicity, to reduce multiplicity to unity. How far has science gone from that generally accepted view of the materialistic school of thirty years ago, that the universe is made up of an indefinite number of atoms, the atoms being our chemical elements! A phrase from one of the most famous of the then leading men of science, Dr. Ludwig Büchner, will mark the greatness of the change: he declared that the carbon atom will always remain a carbon atom, and has been a carbon atom from all eternity; that the hydrogen atom from all eternity has been a hydrogen atom, and to all eternity a hydrogen atom it will remain; for atoms with their properties are indestructible, and are therefore eternal. What man of science would dare to allege that to-day, knowing that he would be laughed to scorn by all his scientific brethren; who would say that these atoms are eternally of the same nature as they have till now been made out to be? What is science in fact, doing as to the atom? It is finding in what is called the atom a composite body, a compound, not an element. This discovery is chiefly due to the researches of Sir William Crookes, who is guided in his investigations by a deeper philosophy of the universe than is common among scientists. It is gradually finding out that these atoms are things that are built up gradually, and that the qualities of atoms are not fixed, but are properties that change with every difference of conditions. Late investigations have shown that when chemical bodies are submitted to extraordinary conditions of cold—such cold as makes the air into a liquid and solidifies hydrogen and oxygen—they suffer the destruction of their supposedly permanent properties. It is proved that, as these conditions are changed, and as lower and lower ranges of temperature are brought to bear upon these chemical elements, one by one their eternal properties disappear, and they lie there changed in their activities, and lose the characteristic traits which enabled them to be discovered as parts of the moving world. Downward and downward falls the temperature, property after property disappears, until science asks, bewildered, what will happen when we reach the absolute zero, what will then become of the properties of matter, what will remain of the characteristics of the elements? Is there not but one Matter, and are not all chemical elements but modifications, aggregations, of this one ultimate matter? Similarly with Force, modern science has made the magnificent generalisation that all the forces that we know are modifications of one Force, and are identical in their essential nature; that heat, and light, and all the various forces around us, electricity, magnetism and the rest, that all these are but vibrations of varying lengths and activities in a subtle medium, and that they may be transmuted the one into the other. They are not fundamentally different, but are one and the same in their root. But if this be so, if there be but one Matter, if there be but one Force, then science is now tending towards unity; and as that unity is traced or aimed at, science will have to pass out of the grosser realm of dense matter into the realm of forces working in subtle media; and we find this wondrous change that, whereas in old days the existence of force was argued for inductively, by studying the changes in matter, now science is beginning to posit the existence of force and to question whether matter is anything more than the action of force. Instead of regarding an atom as a solid indivisible particle, the tendency is to regard it as a vortex of energy, a centre of force. One writer even goes so far as to suggest that an atom is a source "through which an invisible fluid is pouring into three-dimensional space." Other atoms, "anti-atoms," maybe "sinks" through which the fluid pours out. If these unite, may not inertia be neutralised as well as gravity? May there not be potential matter, and may there not be such in space, without any of the attributes which characterise matter, but ready to be vivified and form a system of worlds? Here we have H. P. B.'s atoms and laya centres, put forward tentatively as a scientific problem. Science is mounting into the invisible world and is trying to measure and to weigh that which therein it finds. Now this tendency to unity is the testimony to the One that underlies all manifestation; only one Force, only one Matter; endless diversity of forces, transmutable into each other; endless diversity of forms, which break up again to recombine; only one Force under all forces, one Matter under all forms. It is seen that the very fact of harmony and of evolution points to a root unity, and that eternally independent self-moving particles would only perpetuate a chaos.

As science travels along this most hopeful line, we find great changes are arising in the nature of the studies that are being carried on, and we have that wonderful theory of Sir William Crookes of the genesis of the elements. He takes protyle as a starting-point, which is really Vâyu in its form on this physical plane—Prithivî Vâyu—and out of that builds one atom after another, making all the chemical elements to be bodies aggregated together by the action of a positive and a negative force. Let me just remind you of this, because some amongst you go so eagerly after modern science and despise your own literature. If you had read your *Vishnu Purâna*, with your brain, and not merely with your eyes through modern spectacles, you might have learnt that theory of Sir William Crookes long, long before he gave it. He has drawn a picture, and the picture shows an immovable axis, and around it a spiral coil, and at points in that coil are atoms of the chemical elements, generated by that coil which represents a swinging and cooling force. That spiral is in the great ocean of protyle, or primeval matter, and, as that spiral goes round and round the immovable axis, it generates chemical elements one after another, and so brings into existence the materials out of which the world is to be formed. That is the dry scientific statement summarised from his own address. But I have read in an ancient book of a mountain—which is the emblem of stability, of an axis round which everything is to revolve—thrown into a mighty ocean; and I have read of a great serpent turned round that mountain in spiral coils; on the one side the Suras are pulling and on the other side the Asuras are equally busy. Between the two—the positive and negative of modern science—evolution is started and the serpent spiral begins to turn and turn round that axis. They call the axis Mount Mandara, and they call the spiral coil the serpent Vâsuki while the axis rests on Hari as a pivot; they call the positive and the negative forces the Gods and Demons; and their churning of the ocean gives rise to the materials of the universe. Aye! That is from the seer, who, looking at the ocean of matter, described pictorially what the eyes of the spirit beheld there; while the other is the dry scientific statement of the modern thinker, who works out his magnificent generalisation as the result of his study of the forms. The seer and the scientist have met.

I shall show you, when I come to deal with life, that modern science is coming towards our view of life. I shall give you, from the latest declarations of our modern scientific teachers, points which will show you how they are climbing towards the ancient view which is found in our sacred books; and I will now finish this first part of our subject this morning by one plea addressed to all of you, which I would pray you to think over at your leisure.

There is but One Life, the Life of God, within everything in His universe. No life save His life, no consciousness save His consciousness, no thought save His thought. This is our glory; for inasmuch as we are in His image, we can answer to the vibrations of His thinking, and can reproduce in our minds that which He has initiated in order that we may be evolved. In all the different parts of this universe, different lines of evolution are going on; the sun is doing part of it, the vegetable world another part, the animal world another, the world of man another; but in the world of man there is more diversity, because there Self-consciousness is arising. The final image of the Supreme on earth is man; in man alone is the highest life; the others are climbing towards it, but in them it has not yet evolved. Therefore in man there is more difference; therefore in man, for the time, more separation; therefore in man the great danger of antagonism that the lower kingdoms know not, because they are not sufficiently evolved. Then comes the conflict: I take my own poor reflection of one tiny bit of thought of Íshvara, and I say: "This is Íshvara Himself," and not my poor thought of Him; "Worship this as I see it," that is, "Worship me instead of Íshvara, and my thought of Him instead of Him." So man after man puts up his idea of God as God, and we see all the world divided into many forms of thought and of worship. Then a man imagines that his brother men are worshipping other Gods, and he becomes anxious and troubled, not realising that Gods are many because we are worshipping our own thoughts of God instead of God, our own limited representations instead of the Universal Self. Nay more—I, perhaps, not only say to you that you must worship my conception of God instead of your own, that my knowledge is the limit of manifestation, that my small fancies make up the universe instead of the infinite diversity that alone can represent His might; but perhaps I go further and say: "If you do not worship my idea of God, you are outcaste, you are alien, you belong to a different faith, you belong to a different creed; stand outside; for I am orthodox, you are heretic and blasphemous your faith." So speaks religion after religion, fanatic after fanatic; so one man after another makes his own reflection the God of the universe, and hence antagonises his brethren, whose representations of the divine image are as necessary to its completeness as his own.

That is what I ask you to realise. God cannot be expressed wholly in you or in me, in our miserable limitations, in our poverty of thought, in our wretchedness of impudent assumption. He can only be even partially expressed by all the worlds together; His whole universe is His mirror, and every fragment in the universe gives back to Him, in part His own perfections. Is it not nobler, greater, more glorious, to be a fragment of a perfect whole, making a part of the whole unity itself, subserving it in mirroring Íshvara, than to be shut in with our own fragment of a looking glass, trying vainly to make it perfectly reflect the whole, and refusing any partial reflection of the perfect in our brethren on every side? That is the thought which these lectures will embody, and they will fail in their purpose if they do not carry it home to your minds. For Íshvara, who is Existence and Intelligence, is also A'nanda, Joy, Bliss inexpressible, and that Bliss is only realized when union is consciously accomplished, when the whole is known as one. May I but help you to see the Self in all things: what better service may man do for man?

[SECOND LECTURE.]

THE FUNCTIONS OF THE GODS.

My Brothers :—Those of you who are familia with your own sacred literature will know hov great a part is played therein by those spiritua Intelligences who are spoken of as the Devas, o Gods. As I said yesterday, the existence, the pre sence, and the working of these Intelligences in th administration of nature, in the carrying out of th will of Íshvara, are recognised in every great fait that the world has known. The Hindu speaks c them sometimes as Suras, sometimes as Devas; th Hebrew, the Christian, the Mussulman, speak c them as Angels and Archangels, making the dis tinction between the higher and the lower; th Zoroastrian also recognises their work, speaking c them as Feristhas; and so, in each of the grea religions, we find the presence of these workers i the Kosmos recognised, and we see their function defined. Now it is exceedingly important, especiall perhaps for the Hindu, to understand how wide is th area of their working, how general their functions, for no subject perhaps is more often made a subject for attack by those who desire to injure the ancient religion of India, than the actions of the Gods as detailed in the sacred books. You will continually find that those actions are being misunderstood or mis-represented. The mis-representation, one may always hope, is not deliberate and conscious. It is due to the general materialism of the age. It is due to the fact that men who believe in a religion nominally do not realise the effect of that religion in their consciousness. So that while a man may say that he believes in Angels and Archangels and so on, he leads his life as though they did not exist. Among our Christian brothers there is considerable difference of opinion with regard to these Angels. In the different sections of the great Christian community, the vast majority of those that profess Christianity—making up the old Greek Church, sometimes called the Eastern Christian Church, and those who are numbered in the Roman Communion, the Roman Catholic Church, the two ancient Churches which have preserved an unbroken antiquity and an unbroken tradition from the time of Christ and His Apostles—have maintained and maintain, uninjured and complete, the ancient belief in the ministry of angels. They really lead their lives as

recognising the part that is played in the world t
the angelic hosts, and not only do they regard tl
Archangels as the great rulers of animated nature-
the seven chief Archangels taking the place of tl
seven Gods in other faiths—but they also recogni:
the lower host of angels as concerned continuall
in administering natural laws, in guiding huma
evolution; and indeed they go so far as to say th:
every individual man is in special charge of
guardian angel, who ministers to him from tl
cradle to the grave, who tries to help him i
danger, to advise him in temptation, to protect hi
in peril, to ward off all the evils levelled again:
him, and who, helping him through the gatewa
of death, accompanies him on the other side throug
the invisible world, until he surrenders up h
charge into the hands of Christ Himself. Tl
Protestant communities, however, breaking off a
they did, roughly and abruptly, from the ancier
tradition, full of occult truth, have lost, amon
many other valuable things, this real belief in th
work of the angels. Most members of th
Protestant communities, while they acknowledg
the existence of the angels and vaguely regard ther
as "ministers of God," have no very definite idea c
the part that they play in the world. They do nc
address them, as do the Roman Catholics and th

Greeks. They do not pay them reverence and homage day by day, or look on them as helpers, as intelligences superior to themselves, always willing to render assistance. Practically the angels have passed out of their lives, so far as any conscious realisation of their presence is concerned; and I cannot help thinking that the loss is a very serious loss when you are dealing with spiritual evolution; the whole idea of the Supreme tends to become degraded and anthropomorphised when the intermediate agents are forgotten, and when every petty concern of human life is, as it were, thrown directly under the immediate superintendence of the Supreme. We must not, of course, in recognising the working of the Gods, or the Devas, as I shall call them for the rest of the lecture, lose sight of the unity of the Supreme Deity. We do not, in Hinduism, deny or ignore the existence of Íshvara because we recognise the hosts of the Devas; we do not cloud our belief in the One because we recognise the innumerable hosts of the ministers of His will; there is nothing more against the unity of God in the recognition of the hosts of the Devas, than there is in recognising the diversity of men, yet it is not pretended that we are clouding the unity of the Divine Existence when we recognise the hosts of individuals who make up the whole of humanity. It is mere prejudice or ignorance that makes any one think that because the Hindu recognises the action of the Devas, therefore he has lost his belief in the One Existence beyond even Íshvara Himself, in the fundamental unity that underlies diversity. What he does is, that instead of regarding the world as superintended by an extra-kosmic God, separated as it were from His universe, with a mighty gulf existing between Him and it, he sees in Íshvara the manifestation of the one Life that pervades and sustains all, he sees in Íshvara the one Root out of which all separated existences spring and he sees, stretching between himself and that Supreme, innumerable hosts of Intelligences, step after step, rank after rank, and he looks to climbing up that celestial ladder until he also stands at its very top; for he knows that he also is divine, although as yet in an early stage of evolution, and he recognises the more highly evolved divinity above him, as he recognises the divinity in the stone beneath his feet, in everything that exists in this universe of God.

With that beginning, so that our study may not lead to a misconception, let us pass on to ask what are the functions of these Devas, of these Intelligences, who work in the world. You will at once realise that the functions must be very different, according to the grade of the Devas that we may happen to be studying. Through the whole of the Kosmos they are working. Some are very lofty, some are very little evolved above the level of humanity. One great difference there is between us and them, that whatever may be the grade of their mental, emotional, and spiritual life, they do not, normally, use a physical body. That is a clear mark or line of separation. The being functioning as man, while spiritual, intellectual and emotional, uses a physical body, in order to carry on the activities connected with the physical world. All the hosts of Devas are without that physical covering or vehicle; they normally use as their vehicle a body which belongs to the particular region in the universe in which their normal activities lie. Suppose, for instance, that a Deva belongs essentially to the spiritual world, he will normally use a spiritual body; if he wants to function on the mânasic plane, he will create for himself a temporary mânasic body, drawing together for this purpose the matter of that plane and holding it as his vehicle during the period of his functioning thereupon; if he wants to function in the kâmic region, he will draw together the material of that region and make of it for himself a temporary body;

if he wants to function visibly in the world of man he will draw round himself the matter of the physical plane, and make for himself a body suitable to the immediate purpose that he has in view. So with every other grade. The Devas of the manâsic world use normally the mânasic body, and create the kâmic or physical body as they may want a temporary vehicle. Those of the kârmic region use the kârmic body normally, and create a physical vehicle when they require it. Thus, in every case, the Deva's ordinary body is composed of the matter of the region of the universe to which he belongs; but he has always the power to create any vehicle that he needs for carrying out any purpose with which he is charged. This will perhaps suggest to you one reason for the great variety of forms which a single God may assume. Those whose inner sight is developed, who can see in the regions which to ordinary men are invisible, say that the Gods use many forms. And some of their forms have come down traditionally, described originally perhaps by a great Ṛishi, preserved by his disciples, then thrown into some form of earth, or stone, or metal, painted or sculptured as the case may be; then such an image of the God is handed down generation after generation and represents that Deva under that particular form to his worshippers. We find many forms for one

Deva, just because of the fact that the God makes the form he wants for the particular work he has upon hand, and that none of those forms bind him. They are merely transitory vehicles created for a definite purpose. Some of these forms are indeed relatively permanent, partly because of the worship which is addressed to them. For the Deva will often graciously use a particular form in order to meet the thought of his worshippers. Suppose for instance, taking a lofty example, that Shrî Kṛishṇa willed to reveal Himself to some Bhakta of His, in order that that devotee might have the joy of consciously realising the presence of his Lord, He then most certainly would clothe Himself in the form which that Bhakta was in the habit of worshipping and which drew up the deepest emotions of his heart. For these forms are taken for the very purpose of stimulating devotion, for the very object of attracting the heart by presenting the illimitable Deity in some conditioned form which the concrete mind of man is able more or less to grasp, to understand, to admire and to worship. You cannot love the void of space. You cannot fix your heart on the depths of infinity; you deceive yourself if, with your limited intelligence, untrained even in the lowest forms of Yoga, you think that you can realise Brahman, the Supreme. Too often when we speak of THAT, no real thought responds to our speaking; the lips speak, not the intelligence or the heart. Step by step we have to climb from the manifested to the unmanifested, and, in His compassionate love, God veils Himself in forms of beauty to attract the human heart, in order that the human heart may rise adoringly to His Feet, and that some portion of His life, pouring down thereinto, may enable the Self of the worshipper to realise even partially its unity with Him.

The Devas, then, in their many ranks and divisions, perform functions according to their grade. Speaking generally, their work in the world is to guide evolution according to the design of Íshvara. That really sums up their functions, although we are going to study them in detail. I say nothing of the vast functions of the higher Devas that lie beyond our knowing, beyond the teaching that Ṛishis have given. I deal only with those lower functions that are concerned with our world, and with the solar system of which our world is part. Taking that limitation, suitable to our ignorance, we can study some of the functions of the Gods within the limits of our solar system.

Speaking generally, as I said, that function is to guide evolution, to adapt, to correlate, to carry out the living will of the Supreme, and to carry out that will by bringing together in time and space all the agents and conditions necessary for carrying it out. There is only one supreme Will that guides the universe, and that Will points steadily to progress, to the goal set forth for the universe, the goal towards which it is evolving. Unchangeable, stable, perpetual, that Will knows no swerving; to use a Christian phrase, "there is no shadow of turning" in that immutable Will. The universe rolls along the road traced out by the Divine Will. It cannot be diverted from that road; it cannot change its path; that is the law of the universe, the law on which we rest with faith unshakable. But in the working out of the law in this universe where men are evolving—men in whom is the germ of that same sovereign and imperial Will of God, man being made in the Divine image and containing within himself the germ of the Divine powers—in this universe, as man evolves, wills also evolve which are separate, personal, individual. All the confusion in the world of man is due to this evolution of the separated wills that do not recognise their root in God, but try to follow their own diverse ways, and want to move after their own separated fashions; so that in the world of man, as nowhere else in nature, you have discord instead of harmony, clash instead of peace, struggle and war instead of tranquillity. The world of minerals obeys the com pulsion of the law; the world of vegetables obey: the compulsion of the law; the world of animal: obeys the compulsion of the law; but when mai arises, man in whom the Supreme is to be developec after he has climbed through the lower stages, ii man there awakens the germ of the will, and th separated wills bring about the discord which wil yet end in something greater and richer than th harmony of the stones, of the vegetables, of th animals. For when human evolution is over millions of separated wills will join in one mighty chord of harmonious union, and that union of th wills that voluntarily give themselves is mightie in its powers, more beautiful in its expression, thai compelled obedience can ever be. The music tha humanity sends up to God, in all its varied melody is a far more perfect expression of Divinity thai can be drawn from the monochord that we find ii the lower kingdoms of nature; but you will readil understand that when these warring wills arise something, some one, is wanted in order to adapt to correlate, to bring about equilibrium among th contending forces, so that the one purpose may b steadily subserved. Let me take a concrete illus tration. Suppose I had here a ball which I wan to move. That ball can be moved along a straigh line in innumerable ways. I might give it a single impulse in the direction in which I want it to move; and it would move straight on in that direction following my primary impulse. So would the universe move if it contained only minerals, vegetables and animals, if there were no clashing wills within it, if it were within the iron grip of compulsion, which never in any fashion could be resisted. But I can equally well drive my ball along that straight line, if I know enough of physics, by correlating different and opposed forces. I may send two forces against it at a particular angle, and if my angle be properly measured according to the strength of the forces, then the ball will travel along the same line by the interaction of the two forces as well as by the impact of the one; and I may bring three, or four, or five, or a million forces, to bear upon that ball, and still it will move along that one definite line, if only the forces are calculated and balanced so that their resultant shall always be a force along that straight line. That balancing is one of the functions of the Gods. They take these warring wills, these different directions that are being impressed, as it were, on the rolling world that is going along the road of evolution; they balance, adapt, and correlate them, and thus always keep the world travelling along the straight line, always bringing about the same resultant, the accomplishment of the Will of the Supreme; without them, these wills of ours would work infinite confusion, and the world would never complete its evolution, would never roll upwards to its place at the Feet of God.

We find the Gods discharging other functions which subserve the same purpose. They mould the forms in which the growing life is to express itself. Evolution depends upon the growing power of the unfolding life, but it needs forms whereby that growth shall be carried on. These forms are moulded by the Devas, so that the life, which breaks by expansion its containing form that is out-worn, may have another form into which to go fitted for the capacity that was evolved in the form it has out-grown. We shall find also that they break up forms as well as build them; being always fixed on the one object of serving the evolution of the life. Then again they act as teachers, as guides, as councillors, to those that have gone beyond the normal evolution, that are the first fruits of the human race. Not acting as teachers directly to the masses, they take the more advanced human beings in charge, directly instruct them, test them and try them, as presently we shall see. So that while the general purpose is the helping forward of evolution, this help is rendered in a million ways, according to the needs of the time.

Now, in the past, this working of the Gods was recognised, and the sacred books are full of it. They showed themselves continually among men, they carried on their work, as it were, in the full blaze of day. But now no longer do they show themselves to men at large, and many have forgotten even their existence, and very many people, even in India, materialised by the thought in which they have been trained, are half ashamed to say that they believe in the existence and the working of the Devas. The unbelief makes no difference, save to those who disbelieve. The working of the Gods remains ever the same. They are ever busy in carrying out the Supreme Will. Only they do not show themselves, and to those alone who recognise their existence and their work will they manifest themselves. If in the old days they showed themselves as they do not now, it was because men then had reverence and love and were willing to bow down to those who were wiser and greater than themselves; because then democracy was not reigning; because then the ignorant did not think themselves equal to the learned, nor did man deem himself equal to the Gods. In those days, because they could help they came to the helping; but they will never come visibly again to earth until men have learnt to reverence once more what is above them, and to understand their place in the Kosmos, to worship as well as to command. The Gods work all the same. They are not deprived of their functions by our folly, by our conceit, by our ignorance. Only they work unseen, and we forfeit the sweet comfort of their visible presence, the strength and joy of the old heroic days, the dignity of conscious companionship with the Immortals, the ever-renewed assurance of super-physical life. Not one death that happens on our earth, but a God has struck away that body whose work is over; not one "natural catastrophe," but a God has guided it to the happening; not one help given to a man in need but a God is the agent behind the visible helper; not one answer to the cry of man in his distress that is not the response of a God to human sorrow. Everywhere they are working. Everywhere they are bringing about what we see as dead mechanical nature. Every phenomenon is the veil of a God and there is nothing done in which an Intelligence does not take part.

Seven are the great Gods below the Trinity, below the Trimûrti. Every religion, again, acknowledges these Seven. The Christian speaks of the "Seven Spirits that are before the throne of

God." The Zoroastrian tells us of the seven Ameshaspendas who rule the world. The Chaldean spoke of the seven great Gods. Five only are working and two are concealed, for the universe is in process of evolution and only five stages of it have been reached. Therefore only with regard to five can we definitely speak as to working. The two concealed are beyond our knowing; they are related to future stages of the evolution of the Kosmos. But the five we will now consider. Their names in connection with their functions you know well enough. They are connected with the tattvas of which we were speaking yesterday—the Lord of A'kâsha, Indra; the Lord of Air, Vâyu; the Lord of Fire, Agni; the Lord of Water, Varuna; the Lord of Earth, sometimes called Kshiti (various names are used for him); each of these great Gods has what we may call one region marked out for his working. The matter of that region is the matter in which he works; but in addition to that, each one is represented in the realms of the others by a sub-division on which his impression is especially made. These are the great kosmic planes that I have spoken of, marked off from each other by the tattvas. But if we come down to the physical plane, dealing only with Prithivî Tattva, we shall then find that that is also seven-fold in division and that we have physical solid, physical eartl or Prithivî, physical water or Apas, physical fire o: Agni, physical air or Vâyu, physical ether or A'kâsha Each of these great Gods works on each plan(through the medium that corresponds to the regioı which belongs to him in the Kosmos as a whole How often we see those correspondences as it wer(printed in physical nature. We have light with it: seven sub-divisions as seen in the solar spectrum: showing the seven colours, and the scale with it: seven notes. Colours and notes alike result fron vibrations, and are determined by the number o vibrations occurring in a unit of time. As the universe is built by vibrations, colour and sound are factors of the universe at large, and every region is said to have its own colour; the God of that region ha: his colour—dependent on his vibratory force—whicl he imprints on the region over which he rules; sc that if a Ṛishi looks at the solar system from a higher plane, he not only hears the seven fundamental notes of music, making "the harmony oi the spheres," but he sees a gorgeous display oi colours, as the sphere of every great Deva with hi: own colour interpenetrates the others, yielding an iridescent splendour of interfering radiances, the marvellous "rainbow that is round the throne oi God." Such mystic expressions have lost theiı meaning for the majority, because the sight of those who wrote them is but little developed in these days, and few are they who can see as the seer saw of old.

Each of these great Gods has under him a host of subordinate Gods who carry out his decrees. The constitution of an ordinary state will give you a very good picture of the government of the solar system. We have at the head an Emperor or an Empress; then the officers who represent that supreme authority in separate divisions of the realm; there is the one central authority over the whole, and the officers who wield it in different areas of the Empire. Then these officers are graded in rank, and we have higher and subordinate Ministers, Judges, Magistrates, in descending order, each with a smaller and smaller district to administer, the functions of each becoming more limited as you descend the official ladder; and each responsible to his official superior. That is really a very good picture of the government of the solar system; the head of all is Íshvara Himself; His Viceroys are the great Gods, each with his own vast area over which he rules, and each with his official hierarchy under him, until you come down to the lowest Devas, who carry on the work in the limited area of a village of the solar system.

Such is the outline, then, of the functions. The next thing to grasp is, that, when we see on this plane in which our consciousness is working—the physical plane—any one of these fundamental forms of manifestation, we should try to realise the presence of the God behind the material phenomenon. Not a fire that burns upon the earth whether the fire of the volcanic mountain, whether the fire ranging through the vast forest, whether the fire burning on the household hearth, or on the sacrificial altar, that is not Agni in manifestation with the possibility of his powers coming into visibility. They were not dreamers, they who bade you of old keep safe the fire, the household fire which husband and wife at the bridal kindled, and which, when the life of the married was over in the home, they still carried out into the forest; they carried with them the fire, and it took with them the presence of the God, who through the household life had blessed, had guided, had given prosperity and made the final withdrawal from the household life possible and desirable. That is one of the many truths which modern India is losing.

But when these things were believed in, and the ceremonies connected with them were carried on then nature worked in a definite order, and there were not the same continual irregularities that we have in our modern days. By that harmonious working between man and the Gods, nature answered to man as man answered to nature; while man did his duty, nature in her turn did her duty also; the failure of rain, the failure of crops, the failure of sunshine, the presence of plague, or of any other form of human misery, was seen as having its root in the failure of humanity; and man turned dutifully to that which he had neglected, and thus readjusted the balance which his irregularity had displaced. Let us try and see, as an example, one concrete working in what we call natural evolution. We will turn to the great God Varuna. He works through water; every manifestation of water is his, whether on the physical or on any other plane, in any of the forms that it may take, for what we call "water" is naturally the lowest, coarsest manifestation, his physical body, as it were. He works with it in nature in endless ways—to dissolve, to combine, to dissociate. When we take the greater workings, how very grand is the conception we may gain of the might of the God. Come back with me, far back, into the past, ere humanity had taken form; there see the world as it then was; see how, as fire and water, Agni and Varuna are working on every material to fit the world to be the birthplace of the yet unborn humanity. See how Varuna is working in order to prepare what is wanted of mountain and of valley, of river and of plain; see the might of his work as well as that of his brother Agni, in apparent clash but really in harmony; fire and water meet, explode, and toss up a mountain-chain where before there was none; see how he gathers snow on the mountain peaks, and gradually fills with masses of this snow, frozen into ice, the mountain ravines made by the combined volcanic action; see how the slow ploughing begins; ploughing, ploughing and ploughing again, as the mighty God works onward in the form of glaciers grinding his furrow through the earth, and preparing for the future; see, ages later, how the channel cut out by the glacier is filled by the tumbling cataracts from melted snow, and a turbulent torrent rolls downwards, and against its resistless waves nothing is able to stand; the valley dug out by the plough of the ice is filled with water, and from it the soil is gradually deposited, which in the future will make fertile land for crops in order that man may live. Then Varuna binds his waters into a narrower and narrower channel, until there is mountain range and valley and a river flowing through it: and he carries his river downwards and pours it into the sea and his brother Agni draws it up again to form the clouds. There has come by that mighty action, destructive as it seems in appearance, the building of the plain and the valley where men shall live and love, where children shall be playing, where horses shall graze, where corn shall grow and ripen in the sunshine, and where, on the peaceful banks of the river, men shall worship the God who made possible their happy life.

We talk about the "cruelty of nature." Let us try and understand what this cruelty means. The world now is inhabited. Crowds of men are here, and lo! the river, that made the habitation of the valley possible and keeps it fruitful, now overflows its banks and the mighty flood sweeps away village and town, men, women, children, and cattle, and only desolation is left behind. What is this? Is this horror a divine working? What is this that Varuna has done? Varuna is working for evolution. His thought is not fixed on the forms in which the life is cabined, but on the life that is evolving within them, which can make for itself new forms. When those men are swept away, it is only the breaking of the forms that happens; the life upsprings uninjured and set free; for the body is the prison-house of the evolving life, and if the prison doors were never thrown open, we should be in jail all our lives and make no progress for the future. The God to whom form is nothing and life everything, to whom form is but a changing, convenient vehicle, and the life that moulds the form is the one thing that is worthy of thought, he strikes away the form when its purpose is completed; to him such destruction is the act of mightiest charity it is the deed most helpful to evolution. We err my brothers, when we look on death with eyes that are full of tears, with hearts that are breaking Death is he who brings us to a higher birth, and who sets free the imprisoned soul; it is the liberation of the bird confined within the limits of a cage, enabling it to soar upwards into the heavens singing, as it goes, with joy at the freedom it ha recovered. Does that seem strange? Let us take an illustration from the *Mahâbhârata*:—

There was a council among the Gods in Svarga how some of them would take incarnation upon earth for the sake of helping men at a great crisi in the world's history. Great men were needed and the question arose whether some of the God were willing to bind themselves within the limit of human form, in order to give special help t human progress; among those who were neede for the work that was coming was the son of Som Deva, Varchas, as he was called, and the God desired that this Deva should be born on eart Soma Deva hesitated. He was not willing tha his son should leave him and the heavenly life, and although he finally consented that he should be born as Abhimanyu, the son of Arjuna, it was only on the condition that he should live but for sixteen years, and be killed in the great battle of Kurukshetra. You say, what a strange view of life! What an extraordinary condition for love to make, that this youth should die at the age of sixteen, in the very flower of his dawning manhood, should die a death of violence. Yet that was the will of the one who loved him best, for heaven sees with different eyes from earth. Soma saw the life, and cared not for the form; to a God the form is a prison, death is the gaoler that liberates; hence the condition was made that only for sixteen years might the divine youth live a human life, and then "my son of mighty arms shall come back to me," and that from a battle field, dying gloriously in the midst of the fight.

Do you know that sometimes the swamping of a civilisation by a natural convulsion—such as the going down of Atlantis below the waves of the ocean that we now call the Atlantic, the wiping out of the whole nation or race—is the best proof of love that the Supreme Íshvara through His intermediate agents can show to the lives therein embodied. For there are stages in the world's story where man is so passionately set on a line of action that is against his real progress, when he so determinately sets his desires on objects that hold him back and delay his evolution, that the only mercy that the Gods can show him is to break his form in pieces, and give him as it were a new start for the evolving of himself—the life. Sometimes I have felt, as I have gone through some of the miseries of our great cities in the West, when, in the pursuance of my duty, I have gone with breaking heart through the slums of eastern and southern London, or through those of Glasgow, or Edinburgh, or Sheffield, as I have noted the types of men and women around me, as I have seen the human almost veiled by the brute, and humanity degraded well-nigh beyond possibility of recognition, that no appeal for help was fitting save one that would set free that imprisoned life. I have felt that nothing save the destruction of the forms could give any hope for those imprisoned within them; that for those men and women, as they were degraded, brutal, drunken, profligate, their very forms with the impress of the animal, the best mercy that God could show them would be an earthquake that would swallow the whole great city and set free the lives pent hopeless within it. For not one life would be lost, not one life would pass away, but they would be set free to go into somewhat less unplastic forms and give scope for that divine working towards evolution, which is in extreme cases only possible when the forms, forms of evil, are gone. We speak sometimes of the training of children being easier than that of grown-up people, because they are more plastic. So also the Gods want oftentimes the child-ego in the plastic form instead of in the prison-house grown rigid by age; and they therefore break that environment in order that the young life may grow.

Another great function of the Gods is the dealing with the karma of nations, "collective karma," as it is sometimes called. Suppose a nation is acting in its collective capacity—I am not now thinking of the individuals brought into it by their individual karma but of the nation acting as a unit—and suppose it commits a crime against another nation. There has been one working of karma so tremendous during the last year, that I will take it as an illustration—Spain. Some centuries ago Spain was at the summit of her power; mighty was she among the western nations. There was sent to her, in order to help her forward, the gift of new knowledge. It came truly in a somewhat unacceptable guise, for it came from Arabia, with the stamp of Muhammed upon it; it was brought by the children of Islâm; they brought the light of science with them, and, as they established themselves in southern Spain, they gave that light to Spain. Universities were established. Large classes were formed. From every part of Europe men come crowding to the Schools of Cordova, and there they learnt the beginnings of the Science that has since grown into so mighty a tree in western lands. What did Spain do? Spain called up against these Moors, and against the Hebrews—who also were learned in the learning of the East—the frightful weapons of the Inquisition, the stake, the rack, the dungeon, the torture of exile. Who can count the hundreds of thousands driven out from home, the broken families, the miseries, the poverty and starvation intolerable, which marked the expulsion of the Jews and of the Moors from Spain? Still her karma of success was not complete. Across the Atlantic ocean she sped, Italy lending one of her sons for the glory of the Spanish Empire. In the wake of the ships of Columbus there followed the ships of the conquerors of America, full of Spanish soldiers. I cannot dwell on the story of the conquest of Mexico, and the still more terrible conquest of Peru; I have no time to wring your hearts, as I might, with the tale of the destruction of a great civilisation, of the killing out of the last exquisite traces in Peru of one of the most perfect civilisations that our world has ever known, of the crushing of the gentle Indian race there by chains, by imprisonment, shut out from the glorious Sun whose children their Incas were. Too gentle to struggle, accustomed only to a life of flowers, of music, and of sunshine, they were crammed into caves that they were made to dig in ancient cliffs, dying by thousands upon thousands in the digging out of the gold and silver which their Spanish conquerors demanded, until the very name of the ancient nation perished, and only a few scattered Peruvian Indians remained to represent what was one of the fairest civilisations of the world. Such was the karma made by Spain in the days of her glory, and the horror of her conquests sank into the oblivion of the past. But do the Gods forget? Nay, their memory is perfect. They are the administrators of the divine law, and give the harvest to the sowers. From the very country which they outraged, from the very land that they conquered, a new nation springs up as the centuries go on to take up the old struggle between the two hemispheres, and to-day we have seen America and Spain closing again in the death-grip, but the scale of balance is now weighed down on the other side, and America becomes the karmic agent for working out the woes of the Aztecs and the Peruvians, and for driving from the western hemisphere the nation that there outraged humanity in the centuries gone by. Thus the Gods are needed to bring nations together to balance up these accounts between the races, and so to restore equilibrium once again. Thus they work, using men as their agents, and they bring about these national results. Partly they do it by bringing to birth, at a particular time, men whose individual karma fits them to be the agents of the collective karma of the nation. What was more striking in the Spanish war which has just closed, than the absolute incapacity shown by the men who were the rulers of Spain? Whence came they? They were men who in the past by their individual karma had fitted themselves for the sorry fate of incapable rulers, and they were guided by the Gods to take birth in the families which give rulers to Spain, in order that by their weakness and ineptitude, by their cowardice and their want of foresight, they might serve as men to lead their nation to destruction, the fitting instruments for the working out of Spain's evil karma. See also how at the fit time great men arise to lead a nation to victory. These men are also chosen by the Gods beforehand because of their individual karma, and they are brought to birth in the place and at the time when they are wanted for the working out of the collective karma of a nation. Not by chance is a man brought into the world, not by the compulsion of a dead law, or of a blind necessity; the Gods are working here with an intelligence that foresees and guides, and they choose for the accomplishment of their ends the men whose own karma fits them to be their agents for the work in hand, and then guide them to take birth at the place where that karma can subserve the collective karma of their people.

This also is true in a much more limited way with regard to the working of individual karma. Sometimes you must have wondered how, with all the interfering activities of men, the karmic law could work out with undeviating justice; it is because the Gods are guiding the working. You see somewhere a man who is starving and if you misunderstand karma—as too many of you do, to the shame of India, in a land where this teaching is of immemorial antiquity—you turn aside from that starving man and say that it is his karma to starve and perish; in those hardened hearts of yours you use the will of God as a cover for your own selfishness, for your indifference and your lack of love. That man's karma to starve? Aye, and therefore he is starving! But if a Deva guides you to the place where your brother is starving, it is because he would make you the agent of his beneficence to that man whose evil karma of the present moment has been exhausted by his suffering; the Deva thus says to you: "Man, your brother man is starving, give him the relief it is his karma to receive, and be my agent in carrying out the law." But if you refuse the God, if, blinded by ignorance or indifference, you turn aside and will not carry his message to your brother, he will not for that be thwarted, he will find some other agent, or, as a last resource, he will do it himself by some act that may seem miraculous in the eyes of the blind, for the purpose of the God may not be blocked; but for those who have refused to act as his agents, who have refused to act as his messengers, they have made for themselves the karma of being left unassisted when the hour of their own need shall strike in the future. For the administrators of the good law forget not; every debt is collected, every creditor is paid in full. But you may say that it does not follow that a man's karma is exhausted when you meet him; true, but that is not your business, it is the business of the guiding God, and he will frustrate the physical aid if the karma be still evil. If you have that opportunity given you of making good karma, you have all the merit of your willingness to act, you have all the virtue of your readiness to sacrifice;

but if it is not yet his time to be relieved, you will not find the object of your charity; by circumstances, as you will say, he will have been taken outside your reach. Leave you the Gods to do the work of the Gods, the administration of the law; do you that charity, that love and compassion, which it is ever their will that man should show to man. We cannot break the law; we cannot change their purpose; but we have the choice of co-working or refusing, and on that our individual karma depends.

Then we find further that Devas bring people together and carry them apart, always for the working out of their individual karmas; that men are guided to places and positions at definite times, according to those circumstances which, by their karma, they must meet.

Now men are related especially to one or other of the great Gods, by the constitution of their bodies visible and invisible. That gives them a special affinity for one Deva rather than for another. For instance, the lower hosts of Devas who, we will say, belong to Agni, build into a man's invisible and visible bodies, the kind of matter in which that God normally works. That gives the man a relationship to that particular God. Every man is connected with a special manifestation of God, to whom by his constitution and evolution he should turn. Unhappily ignorance has so widely taken the place of knowledge, that it is difficult for a man to discover to which Deva he is thus related. I have not time to work that out but you will see how thoroughly it supports the ancient idea that men rightly worshipped different manifestations of the Divine, and profited by such worship.

But we must hurry on with this outline, for we have yet to deal with the more highly evolved souls, and on your understanding this last part of our subject will depend your power to defend our sacred literature when it is attacked by those who do not understand it. Therefore I will ask you to follow it carefully, and you can apply the principles that I will illustrate by special stories in a hundred other cases.

The Devas, in their relationship to the more advanced human lives, have that function of teaching that I have alluded to, and also the function of testing and trying them, to see how far they are worthy and reliable, testing all their weak points in order that those weak points may be gotten rid of trying them, where there is a germ of vice still remaining, in order that that germ of vice may be eradicated. Let us try to realise the nature of that working. Suppose we see a man who has made great progress. He is approaching the end of his births. In that man there is some germ of evil still remaining that has not been brought out yet into manifestation by the working of karma. He is going to be liberated, but he cannot be liberated while that germ remains. What shall be done with him? That germ of evil must be hastened to its ripening. It must be made to grow more quickly than otherwise it would grow. It must be gotten rid of, at any cost of pain, of anguish, and of temporary degradation, and the God will take such action as will ripen that germ and bring it to fruitage; so that, the man acting as he would act when that germ had been ripened by evolution, may suffer the results which would follow from the error, and by such suffering may get rid of that evil in his nature, which would otherwise have prevented him from attaining liberation.

Let me give you a story for each of these to make the action clear. You see that a man is strong; well and good; but that strength must be tested to see if there be a flaw anywhere; if there is a rope on which the life of a man is going to depend, he holding it and descending a precipice, that rope must be pulled and tested to see if there be any weak point in it which might break when the man's body is hanging upon it, so that he would fall. There may be a flaw in the rope, and not till it has been tested will the man risk his life upo it. How much less then will the Deva risk th progress of an advanced man on a virtue not stron enough to bear every strain? He will test it wit every possibility of strain, until it has proved itse strong enough to bear the weight which it may b called upon to hold up. We will take our storie from the *Mahâbhârata*, which you all know, or ougl to know. Arjuna was seeking to get divine weapons he was to be a great leader in a battle still in th future. We are at the time of the thirteen year exile, and you may remember that he spent man of these years in the search for these weapon During his search, he sought Maheshvara, wh had promised to give him His own weapon, an he performed many austerities in order that h might come pure into the presence of God. On day as he was performing worship, a wild boar cam along; at the same time a hunter appeared, hunter of a very low caste, a hunter of the hill Now you remember that Arjuna was a Kshattriya and he accordingly caught up his bow to shoot a the wild boar; the hunter also raised his bow t shoot at the wild boar. Two arrows went from th two sides and the boar was struck dead. Arjun was very angry at the interference of this low-cast hunter, and cried: "How dare you shoot at th wild boar which was mine?" and he began to quarrel and to threaten to slay him. Said the hunter: "If you wish to fight, fight"; at that, Arjuna showered his arrows on the hunter but they all fell off from him. The hunter, laughing, said: "Excellent! Excellent! go on! go on!"; and Arjuna hurled at him weapon after weapon, but everything failed. Arrows fell off him, everything broke against him—trees, rocks, everything; he remained untouched and uninjured, until at last He showed Himself as Mahâdeva, and praised the man who had held his own against the God. Thus He tried Arjuna's strength; could he be sent to Kurukshetra with celestial weapons if his strength were too little for the fight? Try him against the Divine potency, limited in order to be faced and fought; when his courage is found to be dauntless and his strength sufficient, then send him to Kurukshetra, tried and proved, able to lead his men to victory.

Take another case, more difficult. Yudhishthira is sad at heart; he is struggling, has failed, and is in danger. Drona is there, leading the hosts of his enemies, and he has been driven by him from the battle-field. No one is able to stand against Drona; every one flies before the face of that mighty warrior; he turns back every attack. What can be done? Yudhishthira is in despair. Is he to be conquered?

A stainless king was this son of Pându, one of th noblest and most blameless figures that ancien literature paints; but with a strain of weakness i: him which in critical times would sometimes sho a too great readiness to yield, too little of th Kshattriya's power of standing alone against an force that might be brought to bear against him a little germ of weakness was there, that had in : the possibility of a fatal fall. Shrî Kṛishṇa : there, the great Avatâra, and Bhîma comes rushin up from the battle-field saying that he has slain a elephant, whose name is the same as the name c the son of Drona. If Drona hear that his son Ash vatthâmâ is dead, he will drop his weapons, he wi let go his enemy; no further will he fight when h: beloved is gone. "I told him that Ashvatthâmâ wa dead, but he would not believe me; he sent me t you saying that Yudhishthira is a devotee of trutl he will not tell a lie for the sovereignty of the thre worlds. If he says Ashvatthâmâ is dead, I wi believe." Terrible is the strain; mighty the forc brought to bear against the man who has a weal ness in him; and Shrî Kṛishṇa, standing by hin watching him steadfastly, advises him to utter th: which is not true. God advises this almost blam less man to tell a lie? How strange the scen Yudhishthira, yielding to Shrî Kṛishṇa, tells tl falsehood, and Drona lets fall his weapons and is killed. If the story stopped there, we might well be puzzled. If Yudhishthira's life was no further told, we might well ask: what is this that we have studied? But when we remember that one of the great functions of the Teacher, the Gurudeva, is to bring out any weakness inherent in His pupil, because otherwise that weakness will keep the man tied, and he will not be fit to be liberated, we pause and read on. When that lie was spoken, the chariot of Yudhishthira sank downwards to the ground, no longer able to support itself, truth having been violated. And as years went on, the bitterness of that memory of a falsehood remained; the sorrow of the slaying of the preceptor by a lie ate deep into the heart of the king; he never recovered from it, he never got rid of its effect; over and over again, he breaks from his repose in anguish; "I have slain my Guru." The sorrow worked and the shame, till the anguish purified that noble soul from the last stain of weakness; and when the Great Journey is over, when wife and brothers lie dead behind him and he utters not a word of protest against the death of his beloved, when he stands ready to ascend to heaven, when only one living creature remains with him, the dog who had followed after him faithfully through all his wanderings since he left his capital, when that dog remai ed his sole companion, trusting his master's lo faithfully unto death, then comes down a migh God and stands beside him. "Your time has com mount on my celestial chariot, and ascend in yo body unto the heaven where you have won tl right to sit and reign." Will he now yield to tl invitation of the God? He said: "This dog is her he has trusted to my protection and I cannot lea him alone; I must take him with me." The G answered: "Dogs have no place in heaven; do are unclean, no place for them is there; you ha left your dead brothers behind, and your wife wh she perished; why should you remain still with th dog?" "They are all dead," he answered "f the dead, the living can do nothing. This creatu is still living and has sought my protection; I w not abandon him." "Nay," the God said, "be n so foolish; leave the dog there." But Yudhishthi stood firm; he was strong enough to stand again the God, and to show righteousness and fidelity the poor brute that had placed his love in hin unless he might take the dog with him, he wou stay on the earth and do his duty. Such lesson had l learnt from his fall; such is the result of the workir of Shrî Kṛiṣhṇa on his evolution. We can see th same working throughout the whole of that strugg

Trace Shrî Kṛiṣhṇa through the pages of the *Mahâbhârata*, and you will find that He never deviates from one steady purpose—to bring the great struggle to a foreseen ending, where justice shall triumph and the Kshattriyas of India shall disappear; He was at once destroying injustice and preparing for the future of India, breaking down the iron wall of her warring caste that ringed her around with safety. There is a particular aim in everything that He does, and you will see that His purpose is immovable, if you study carefully. He is working towards its accomplishment the whole way through. Look at the way in which He steps in when His strength or protection is needed; see how He tries to stimulate the Pândavas to do their duty, and only takes their place when they fail. See the case where Shrî Kṛiṣhṇa having promised that he would do no battle, Arjuna falters before the face of Bhîshma and has no heart to strike; you remember how sad was the struggle. Arjuna was not able to strike harshly at Bhîshma, the greatest of all men and all warriors, perfect in Dharma, the grandsire and the teacher of all. "How can I slay him?" insisted Arjuna; "I remember when as a child soiled with dust, I climbed on to his knees and throwing my arms around him called him 'Father,' and he said to me, 'I am thy father's father.' How can I bring myself to slay him?" And you will remember how Shrî Kṛishṇ Himself told him not to shrink, 'bade him sla him.' Hard was the task; Arjuna's memory wa too strong for him; he only fought in appearanc with restrained might, not with vigour, until a last Shrî Kṛishṇa saw that He must stimu late this man to do his duty, and to fight, thoug it were against his old teacher himself; H throws down the reins of His horses, takes th whip, and leaps down from the chariot, and wit the whip He rushes through the brunt of the battl to attack Bhîshma Himself. Ah! that sight is har for Arjuna; it appeals to him as Kshattriya, an duty is remembered instead of emotion; throwin his arms round Shrî Kṛishṇa to stop him he says "Go back! Go back! and drive me yet again, and will do my duty even to the slaying of Bhîshma. Now what does that mean? It means that the purpos of the God will be accomplished, whether or not man is found to do it; that evolution will procee no matter who may falter or who may hinder; tha while evolution will go on under the Will of God individual progress depends on individual co operation with that Will; that God evolves His agent by setting them to His work, and that their progres depends on the extent to which they are able t receive the impulse that He imparts. Only on other case I will take to show you how Shrî Kṛiṣhṇa worked when the force was too great for Arjuna to meet, when He saw Arjuna could do nothing with all the valour at his command, that no force of appeal, no stimulus, could enable him to defend himself. One weapon was thrown that might not err in its aim, one weapon a celestial weapon that He had given as a boon, when He waked from His thousand years of sleep. That weapon was cast against Arjuna. Arjuna could not avert it. Alone of all the weapons in earth and heaven, that weapon must go to its ending, and Arjuna would have been slain in the midst of the battle. What can be done? He could not cut it with the arrows from Gâṇdîva, he could not use against it any of the mighty weapons that the Gods had given him. This was the weapon of the Supreme, which nothing was able to oppose. Shrî Kṛiṣhṇa then, at that last moment, as the weapon flies straight at the breast of the warrior throws Himself in front, and, as it strikes His bosom, it knows its Master and is changed into a garland of flowers. So also with the chariot on which He drove. He bade Arjuna first get down. He bade him take his weapons, and until Arjuna had left it, Shrî Kṛiṣhṇa stood there immovable, He would not stir; and the moment He left it the whole chariot burst into flames, for only His presence had kept it together, He who was the Lord of fire as well as the Lord of all else. You see, my brothers how fruitful is the study of this subject, when you are dealing with the sacred literature; how you may be able to explain it to men of your own faith and defend it against the attacks of men of other creeds. Do not defend it with bitter words, do not defend it with harsh language, do not defend it with wrath in your mind, and indignation making your tongue poisonous; but remember that where ignorance attacks, it is the duty of knowledge to defend; and that when that which ignorance attacks is the spiritual food of millions, every man of knowledge should spring forward to defend it lest the ignorant of that faith should swerve, when they see the truths in their books assailed by those who do not understand.

That then is the outcome of this lecture. I ask you to remember that in every stage of your life Gods are around you. No karma that you make that they will not remember; no appeal that you utter, that they will not answer. If for a moment no answer seems to come, or if sorrow that you shrink from falls upon you, remember that the hand of love allows it thus to fall, and that in bearing that sorrow bravely, you are swiftly working out your own deliverance. You are to be men, not children, in the future; men-sons of the living Íshvara whose image you are, and not babies that He must for ever carry in His arms. He asks from you the strength of men to help the Gods. He is evolving you as the agents for His future universe. You may delay, if you will. You may lose time, if you will. Kalpa after Kalpa, you may remain at a low stage. If so you choose, He will not force your will; but your wisdom lies in letting His Will work in you to your swift and perfect evolution, that you may have the joy of carrying out that Will in other worlds, of consciously being His agents under other conditions; for men are Gods in the making, and we are preparing to discharge the functions of the Gods.

[THIRD LECTURE.]

EVOLUTION OF LIFE.

MY BROTHERS,—We have reached a point in ou study from which we may begin to trace the Evolu tion of Life in our own system; that evolution take place on the various planets, but it is similar in it general outline, though modified in its details on th different globes. We shall chiefly confine ourselve to our own world and our own humanity; at th outset we shall be obliged to go somewhat furthe afield, but for the greater part of our study we ma confine ourselves to the evolution of life on ou earth. Now we are seeking in our study to find common ground of agreement on which co-operatio may arise between peoples of different faiths and o different schools of thought. If we are trying t find a meeting-place for western and for easter Science, if we are seeking in the light of Religio to understand some of the mysteries of life, it i right and fitting that we should remember that n one religion has a monopoly of truth, and that an one who is seeking to expound the truth should be able to fortify his position from the different religions of the world, and to show that on all great, essential, and fundamental truths they speak with a single voice, they teach an identical lesson. Therefore in dealing with my subject this morning, I shall, as before, draw your attention on the main points where challenge might arise to the consensus of religious opinion, to the definite statements of the world's Teachers; so that the tendency towards unity, on which the future evolution of life depends, may be helped to develop amongst us. And there is a special reason for that just now. We shall see, as we trace out the evolution of life, that we are in the very crisis of the intellectual evolution, and we shall find that the characteristic of that stage of evolution is division and separation, and the placing of the individual apart from, and somewhat in conflict with, other individuals. And we shall find that the next stage in the evolution of life is the seeking for union amid the individualised units; that the next divine aspect that man has to develop in the Self within him is the aspect of union and not the aspect of diversity; and it is of importance that those who are seeking the light, those who are striving to co-operate with nature by understanding her hidden ways, should realise the next step of evolution as well as the present, in order that they may co-operate with nature by themselves taking that step, thus quickening the possibility of similar taking for all mankind.

Now with regard to life in its relation to forms, a change at the present time is coming over the thought of western Science. I pause on this for a moment in order to substantiate that assertion, for it is important in the search for the means of drawing together the two kinds of science, ancient and modern, to notice how much the position of the leading scientists of the West has been modified with regard to life and form during the last ten years. I take as a declaration on this subject of life, issued some years ago, the article on Biology in the last edition of the *Encyclopædia Britannica*, written, as all the articles in that *Cyclopædia* are written, by a prominent man in the scientific world. In dealing then with life, the writer of the article in question distinctly states that "a mass of living protoplasm is simply a molecular machine of great complexity, the total results of the working of which, or its vital phenomena, depend, on the one hand, upon its construction, and on the other, upon the energy supplied to it; and to speak of 'vitality' as anything but the name of a series of operations is as if any one should talk of the 'horologity' of a clock." That is to say, that to regard life as being in any sense a common existing principle, as anything more than a mere succession of phenomena in connection with a particular apparatus of matter, is as foolish and unreasonable as if, looking at a clock, you should separate its going property from the mechanism of the clock itself. A purely mechanical view of nature is thus taken, and life-processes are regarded as being due to the unstable equilibrium of protoplasm; the series of these life-processes is brought about merely by mechanical and chemical changes, the actions called vital being thus mechanical in their character. But at the last meeting of the British Association, the President of the Chemical Section—chemistry having been the very science to lead the scientific world towards materialism in this respect—has taken up an entirely different standpoint, a point that brings the question into a line with ancient thinking, and that starts the investigations of western Science along a road whereon the most fruitful results are likely to be encountered. Dr. Japp, the President of that Section, compares the action of life to the action of an operator who is deliberately working with a purpose, using knowledge and will in order to bring about a definite result. "The operator," he says, "exercises a guiding power which is akin, in its results, to that of the living organism," and going on to explain in very technical language th ground on which this view is based, he conclude by saying: "Every purely mechanical explanatio of the phenomenon must necessarily fail. I see n escape from the conclusion that at the momen when life first arose a directive force came into pla —a force precisely of the same character as tha which enables the intelligent operator, by th exercise of his will, to select one crystallise enantiomorph and reject its asymmetric opposite. That is the declaration: that with the arising o life there is an arising of consciousness which exercises a directive force in nature, as we see it exercising a directive force in the choice exercised by men Put those two statements side by side, see the entir reversal of the attitude, and then you will be abl to measure to some extent the change that ha come over western thinking—the recognition of lif as identical with consciousness, a position whicl has ever been taken in the hoary Science of th East.

Now let me, before going into details, sugges to you the path that we are to follow. From th One Existence, that One without a second, arises as we saw in our first study—Íshvara, God in Hi creative and manifested aspect, Íshvara clothed i

Mâyâ, out of which a new universe is to be builded. Threefold we found Him to be in His manifestation, threefold in the aspect that He showed forth; so that a Trimûrti, or Trinity, is the aspect towards this universe of the manifested God; His working will show this triple character, and the evolution of life is threefold, whether we study it in nature or in man. I know the thought that arises in many of you, accustomed to the broad statements in eastern literature. You think of the building, the sustaining, and the disappearing of a universe. Perfect, you say, is the One Existence, infinite, unchangeable; perfect in the ending is the universe, as perfect in the beginning; why then this long evolution of life with all its struggles, with all its imperfections gradually and slowly transcended. Why from the perfect should the imperfect come forth? Why should it be trained into perfection, and then return into that perfection whence it came? That question is based on a fundamental misunderstanding which it is necessary to correct; a misunderstanding which never could have risen amongst you if the Scriptures had been read in the light of the Yoga-developed consciousness, and if the broad outline which is presented had been followed out carefully in thought so that its stages might be marked. You will remember how it is written in the *Chhân-*

dhogyopanishad that the One willed to multiply and the moment you grasp the idea of multipli cation, if you think of what it means instead c merely repeating the word, you will realise tha multiplication must necessarily mean division an therefore limitation, and that limitation necessaril implies imperfection. But having gone so far, yo would then have proceeded to ask: By what word is the universe described, and what idea is hidde beneath the words? And you would find that whe God is spoken of as a Fire, the universe is not spoke of as a Fire, but as a spark, and the lives of men a described as millions of sparks that come from th illimitable Fire. Not only is that word "spark used, showing you the limitation that comes wit manifestation, giving you the idea that the spar fed by suitable fuel is to be developed into the lik ness of the Flame whence it came; but as the spa is of the same nature as the flame, so we are to "Thou art That," the Self in man is identical i nature with the Self that gave it birth. You wi remember another word which is constantly used describe alike the universe as a whole, and also th parts of which it is composed—the word germ or see Let me ask you to turn to the *Bhagavad Gîtâ*, familiar to every student amongst you, and to liste for a moment to the words chosen by Shrî Krishn when He desires to convey the idea of the nature of the universe, and its relation to the Supreme What does He say?

> Mama yonir Mahad Brahma tasmin garbham dadâmyaham.
>
> Sambhavasarva bhûtânâm tato bhavati Bhârata

"I place the germ in the womb of Mahad Brahma." What do these words imply? for the whole turns on our understanding of that word "germ." Mahad Brahma is the matter of the universe, vivified by Brahman in His third aspect—that which Theosophists call the Third Logos, which in the Trimûrti is spoken of as Brahmâ. Looking on Brahman as the *One*, Mahad Brahma is the third aspect of His revealing, which vivifies and makes atomic the matter of the universe, the womb of the seed of the Eternal Life. In that, brought into manifestation by Brahmâ, or the Third Logos, the Second, the generating Father, Vishnu, places that germ of life that therein it may develop; not Himself in all the might of His Deity, not Himself in the force of His unfolded powers, but the seed of His life—capable of evolution, containing everything within it potentially, but showing forth nothing in manifestation at the beginning of the universe. True, the child is the father revived; true, the child is the same as the father. None the less, the life which the father gives is the seed containing t power of development, and the universe is but the se of Deity, with every power involved within it, a capable by its evolution of becoming the image of t Supreme: none the less is every power germinal, n developed, potential, not actual; only at the endi will that seed, grown into perfect manhood, sh forth the image of its generating Sire, and give a n Íshvara to the future from whom further univers may evolve. That is the answer to the questio Why this long evolution? It is this evolution th we are to trace from the germ to the perfect, l given as germ to grow to the God.

Let us look first at the matter in which this life to be clothed—not in detail, that is to-morrow's wo —but just as to the principle involved in the evol tion of the matter through which the life is to expr itself. We heard the first day about tattvas. V found that they were modifications of Prakriti, t primary matter, brought out one after the other the regions of the universe were builded. All th we need for our purpose this morning is to reme ber that five of these are concerned with the prese evolution, that the highest of these is the A'kâsha the highest sense of the term, then Vâyu, then Ag then Apas, then Prithivî; all these are kosmic a they represent vast planes in the universe, but ha their correspondences in the physical globe—ether, air, fire, water, earth, these being only the reflections in miniature of their great prototypes in the system at large. The only other thing we need to remember this morning with regard to matter, is that the whole of these are animated by the life of the *third* aspect of God. Here is a point where we may pause for a moment and look at other religions, and we shall find that they all tell us exactly the same. Not only do we find in Hinduism, in such a book as the *Vishnu Purâna* that the Divine creation was from Mahat—the third manifestation—that these great tattvas were evolved by modifications from the principle of individuality which is the characteristic of that aspect; but if we turn to the Hebrew teachings we shall find that it is distinctly stated that the "Spirit of God," the third aspect, or Wisdom, moved on the face of the waters. Translating the symbol of water we have matter; it is so used in every great religious scripture, and when it is said that the Spirit of God moved on the face of the waters, we have the picture of a brooding life, brooding over and permeating the ocean of primeval matter, giving to it the life that will enable it to serve as the womb for a higher life; the divine energy that thus vivifies matter comes from the third Person of the Christian

Trinity. That Hebrew statement dominates tl whole of Christendom, inasmuch as the Christi: Churches take the older part of their scriptures fro the hands of the Hebrew people; and in quotii that, I am not quoting it only as an authority fro the Hebrews but as including the authority of tl whole of Christendom, bound by that Hebrew teac ing. I might show you, did time permit, that oth great Teachers have spoken in the same sense; tl outcome being that the matter in which evoluti(is to take place—of which our world of organisn including our own bodies, is to be formed—th matter is permeated by the Divine life, and tl aspect of Divine life that permeates it is that of tl third manifestation of God. That is the fund mental reason why Brahmâ is no longer worshippe That is why no temples are raised to Him and wl worshippers do not throng to His shrines. H work was dominant in the earlier stages of tl universe, but is now overshadowed by the workii of another aspect of the mighty God, Vishnu Preserver, as Sustainer, and as Organiser. He the life which is active in all organisms; and tl life which animates the atoms of matter havii been given and partially evolved, the continuii aspect of that work is hidden at the present sta; of the universe; the main evolution of life th is now occurring is carried on and directed by other aspects of God.

Sometimes in theosophical literature, that vivification and building up of matter is spoken of as the work of the first great life-wave in the solar system; as a wave rolling forth so does the life of God go forth for the building of the atoms whereof the system is to be composed. The critical point is this: that the life is veiled over and over again in a five-fold involution; we find it said that Prâna five-fold divides itself, for five are the types of the atoms, five are the great divisions of the materials, and in each successive type, the previous type permeates and encloses it, as we found we could read in the *Vishnu Purâna*, dealing with the building up of the tattvas. (It will be remembered that the types are really seven, but that two are concealed.) One important result comes from this which I will deal with more fully to-morrow, that the form—being built up from matter containing within it this involved and concealed life—has the power of unfolding to the highest possibility of the life thus concealed. Sheath after sheath is made in order that sheath after sheath may be brought into activity as a vehicle of the Self, and that five-fold ensheathing for the human Self is wrought in order that it may have a vehicle capable of responding to evei vibration that it sets up or that it receives. A the vibrations become subtler and subtler in the character, sheath after sheath becomes active ar responsive, and enables the life to function exte nally by means of the sheath. Let us however tui —for that will be fully worked out to-morrow— the next great life-wave with which we are co cerned; it is the life of the second aspect of Deit spoken of in Hinduism as the life of Vishnu, spoke of in Christianity as the life of the Son of God l whom all things were made. As that life outpou into the universe prepared to receive it, as that li begins to draw together the matter which, vivifie by the first out-pouring, is now ready to respor to the vibrations of the life that organises and su tains, vibrations are sent out by this Divine Li into the higher regions of the universe, beginnir the task of drawing the matter together into form The earliest stages of these are the ante-types what shall be in evolution—not such forms as w speak of in the lower world, concrete objects whic can give rise to concrete ideas, but that which dim we are trying to reach in the mind to-day, whe we abstract from a great class of concrete objec its uniting quality, its common characteristic, ar formulate this apart from the objects themselve

I have sometimes taken the triangle as the very simplest image which thought can form. You may have triangles of any size, you may have triangles of almost any shape, provided only three lines are used, and those lines are right lines, or unbent. What is the governing characteristic of the triangle? That its three angles, formed by the meeting of enclosing sides, must be equal to two right angles. Now supposing that you have the power of brain, the power of abstraction, to take ten, twenty or thirty concrete triangles and hold them in the mind as though you were looking at them in outer form, to create their mental images so that every form is present in your mind, you directing your attention to them all at the same time, then—if out of these many concrete objects that have the particular properties in common of the three right lines that enclose and the sum of the three angles equalling two right angles—if you can draw out the idea of that common property, separated from every concrete triangle, and make it an object in consciousness, then you will have risen from the concrete to the abstract, and will have some idea of what is meant by an archetype in the higher world. The earliest actions of the Deity in evolving a system are of this nature; He generates certain types or archetypes, and by the sub-division and multiplication of these the whole universe of con crete objects is formed; each one of them is capabl of generating innumerable forms that reproduc its own characteristic amid endless diversities c subsidiary properties.

It is not without interest that some of our scien tific men have tried to find unity amidst diversit) and to discover the types of the animal kingdor amid the innumerable diversities of the separate animal forms. One of the most famous of thos men, Sir Richard Owen, tried to formulate a archetype which should represent every fundamen tal characteristic of the vertebrate, like no particula vertebrate but showing forth the qualities presen in every vertebrate; he worked this out from a stud of vertebrates, setting aside the characteristics i which they differ and synthesising into a singl form the qualities possessed by all. The revers process is what really occurred; the archetyp which came forth from the Divine Mind generate in the world of matter myriad different types i each of which it is itself expressed. That gleam c genius which illuminated the mind of the moder scientist is interesting as a ray from the conceptio of creative action given in our sacred literature and you will find, if you study carefully, that th earliest forms are not concrete objects but gener

tive powers, and that these coming forth from God make models for the future types, each type being related to its ante-type, each concrete object to its abstract idea. Thus also the Greeks taught, Pythagoras and Socrates and Plato; thus also many of the Hebrews taught, the doctors of the Kabala; and both the Greek Philosopher and Hebrew Kabalist have declared that the visible world of objects could never have come into existence had not the invisible world of Ideas preceded it, so that the objects repeated in multitude what an Idea presented in unity. That Idea thus coming forth from God and drawing to itself forms in subtle matter, produces the types of forms that are gradually to be worked out in evolution; and those of you who have studied the *Secret Doctrine* of Madame Blavatsky may remember that the archetypal world is therein spoken of as the first which is created, and as that on which the whole of the evolution of denser worlds depends. It is made of the A'kâsha which contains within itself the possibility of all forms as we are told, and these Ideas are drawn forth and reproduced in greater detail by the Builder on the A'kâshic correspondences of Agni. Life is evolved by the modifications in consciousness which Íshvara brings about; the modification in the consciousness of Íshvara preceding the moulding of the matter. As that life-wave descends int denser and denser matter, it draws together mor and more separate forms, that become denser i their nature, until at last, through kingdom afte kingdom, it comes down to the mineral form where life is most restricted in its operations, wher consciousness is most limited in its scope. This i the process of the involution of life in matter, th descending arc. From this lowest point the lif ascends, revealing more and more of its power and ordinary western "evolution" begins here, th earlier process being ignored.

How did that Divine life and consciousness, in th first upward stage of evolution, evolve in the germina life the power to respond? The life within the ston has the capacity to respond, but in a very limite fashion, partly owing to its germinal nature, partl owing to the rigidity of its surrounding vehicle therefore the brooding life of Vishnu, nourishin this germ, at once stimulates it by impacts from with out and gradually modifies the rigidity so as to mak progress possible. Long, long remains the life im bedded in this rigid material, working from withi outwards, as all life works, playing upon and thu softening the rigidity, and slowly giving the forı more plasticity in response; we can sum up th whole of the working of the life, as the receiving (

vibrations from matter without and the answering of vibrations from itself within. Notice in the earliest stages how tremendous are the impacts; if you go back to the time when the world knew not humanity, how gigantic are the operations of nature showing herself in her mineral forms; earthquakes, eruptions, crushing and grinding of materials, disintegration and reconstruction, all on the mightiest and most gigantic scale; under all that, the life, trying to make the matter more plastic and able to answer more readily; and inasmuch as there is life, there is consciousness, *i.e.*, the power to respond, that power is developed within it, stimulated by the brooding life of Íshvara. He dwelling within, and enveloping and permeating all objects, makes the seed of life extend and grow by his nourishing warmth, that it may become finally an independent centre. We see the life within the stone beginning to vibrate more actively as these tremendous blows come upon it from without; and mass is thrown against mass, and mountain is piled upon mountain, until at last these mineral materials gain larger power of transmitting impulses to the life within; the impulse coming through more strongly because of the lessened opposition from the form, the life responds more actively and begins to evolve, developing more definitely the power of response. As this process is repeated over and over again, the life within the minerals vibrates with ever increasing rapidity, and the matter yields to it with ever greater readiness, until a stage of plasticity is reached at which the beginnings of the vegetable world can be brought into existence. Between mineral and plant in the lowest stages no definite dividing line can be drawn by science. So general is this absence of dividing lines in nature that a separate kingdom has been recognised as including low types of both vegetable and animal, and between the vegetable and mineral kingdoms a class is recognised in which the rigid crystal which belongs to the mineral kingdom has become the plastic crystalloid that belongs to the vegetable; maintaining the outline of the mineral form, but showing the plasticity of the vegetable, and thus yielding far more readily to the moulding influences of the life within. The life thus encased in more plastic material receives vibrations from without more easily and responds more strongly, until in the ascent that it is beginning to make, it adds the early beginnings of a power of consciousness that in the mineral was not present. We call it sensation: the power of feeling pleasure and pain, the power of responding to the outside impact by a feeling within the life. After the life in the mineral has developed the power of response, then the next stage in evolution is that the response takes on the sensations of pleasure and pain, appearing as that within the life which responds severally to harmonious or discordant impact from without. As the life develops this power of sensation, progress becomes more rapid. The animal kingdom is gradually builded and the power of sensation is the great characteristic which is developed through that kingdom, until—the animal forms having been rendered plastic through many ages by the impulse of life, and the life having formed and strengthened the power of responding by pleasure and pain to harmonious and discordant vibrations—the next stage is ready to be taken, the building of the vehicle for man.

That outer body in which man is to dwell resembles closely in its nature, in some of its fundamental characteristics, the animal bodies which the life had vivified before man was called into existence. "Out of the dust of the ground," says the Hebrew scripture, God formed the body of man, a symbolic way of saying that out of the material that had made the lowest forms of life, was also to be made the outer coating of that vessel, into which a new flood of Divine life was to be outpoured, forming the human Self, or Spirit. We learn, when we study occultism, that this third outpouring of Divine life comes neither from the Third, nor from the Second, but from the First Logos, therefore called Mahâdeva, the Great God, the Supreme. From Him comes the third impulse which is to complete evolution, the third outpouring of life, that only accomplishes its final evolution in this age by methods of Yoga; therefore is He often represented as the great Yogî, the great Guru, under whose instructions the latest stages of evolution are to be carried out. When that life-force comes down, and the human Self is sent forth to occupy its tabernacle, the ancient process is again repeated, and it is only the germ of the highest life that is given and not the completed life. Round it are vehicles that are able to respond, round it are vehicles that have the power of developing more highly, that are already capable of sending in vibrations arousing feeling in the life that they enclose, and now—enwrapped by the life of Vishnu—this germ of the Divine Self begins to stir and live as man.

At first there comes from it very little response to the life that is transmitted, very little answer to that which is outside; but what are the characteristics of this infant Self, this spark of the Eternal Fire? Triple in aspect is the life in man as it is triple in the Deity, and its characteristics are the same, Sat, Chit, Ananda. We speak thus of Brahman, and if we study the human Self we shall find these three aspects present also in that human Self; and the first to develop in man, as in the Kosmos, is Chit or knowledge. All the earliest stages of human evolution have to do with the evolution of Intelligence; it is that with which we are now concerned, as we climb this mighty ladder. We are evolving intelligence or intellect, and if we trace its stages from the earliest germs as they appear in the primeval races of the humanity of our globe, and as fostered in those races by the Great Ones who came to us as Teachers from other worlds, we shall find that the dawning intellect in man was but very slightly responsive to anything that came to it from without, and that at first every effort of the intelligence was stimulated by the promptings of the animal nature, by the sting of desire, by the passions which belong to the animal part of man. Consider a savage. When is a savage active? Only when some animal desire awakens within him. If he is hungry, yes, then he will begin to think, "where can I find food?" If he is thirsty, he will ask, "where shall I find liquid?" Any animal prompting that arises within him, his dawning mind applies itself to satisfy; and the germ of mind is stimulated by the promptings of animal desire. In that stage he knows not right from wrong;

right and wrong for him have no existence; hunger and thirst, sexual desire, and the need for sleep, these are the things that make up his life and that move his dawning consciousness; these only are strong enough to stir it into activity; it cannot yet initiate activity from within. But as these play upon it, life after life, birth after birth, century after century, in successive incarnations of this germinal but growing life, as these vibrations continually arouse, awaken the life of the intelligence, which is the third aspect of the Self, these repeated vibrations, repeated over and over and over again a thousand times, by that very repetition bring about an internal tendency to repeat it again without a fresh stimulus from outside; and we find in the next stage of the evolution of intelligence, still in the savage, that the savage does not wait for hunger in order to search for food, but that the memory of hunger and the memory of food are enough to send him out, before the hunger strikes him, in search of the meal that to-morrow he will require to satisfy the needs of the body. But what a change is there if we consider it, small as it is in appearance. The man is no longer stimulated by an outer impulse coming from the animal nature; he is stimulated by a mental image, a connected picture of the painful state of the body wanting food and of the food which is able to change that state into one of pleasure; that is, he is now able to form mental images, and these stimulate him into activity. How great the change! No less than a change of the centre of consciousness from the animal to the human, one of the most significant changes in the evolving life. Now, for the first time, he does not wait to be pushed from without. He begins action from within, and the body obeys the impulse that comes from the centre, instead of the impact that strikes the centre from without. Now evolution becomes more rapid, for as this great change, one of the hardest of changes, is made, the intellect in man begins to cognise itself, and Self-consciousness begins to arise. Separation is recognised between its own centre, that thinks, and the things outside that make it think; the "I" and the "Not-I" arise, and the centre begins to shape itself and to be capable of growth.

How shall the growth go on? By conflict. This is the characteristic of the intellect. It has to make the "I" a strong centre, a separate centre, otherwise no further evolution is possible. You may say that this looks like going downwards; nay, it is the germ of a new centre of life in which Divinity itself shall unfold when evolution is complete. There must be a clearly defined centre of consciousness, else how shall it work onward to perfection? An(that centre grows by struggle. All strength come: by struggle of one kind or another. If you wan your arms to become strong, it is no good to lie on : sofa and leave the muscles to grow merely by th nourishment that you give them. They want mor than nourishment, they want exercise; and it is th law of all growth of form that the life must b drawn into the form, for only then can the form ex pand and become capable of receiving a furthe impulse of life; if the muscles are to grow, the cell that compose them must be stretched by exercis(and the life must flow into the expanded cell only then does it become capable of multiplicatior so that there may be many cells where befor there was only one. The difference between th weak man and the strong man, the man who i feeble and the man who is athletic, is the differenc brought about by exercise and struggle, by pullin against resistance, by taking up a weight an whirling it round and making the muscles strai against the weight. That is a picture of the wa in which all life is working for development of form the impulse of life leads to the exercise of the forn the exercise makes it plastic and increases the forn through which the life is thus enabled to flow mo1 largely. That is as true in the mental world as i the physical world; for the mental world is also a world of phenomena. It is not the One; its characteristic is diversity, each being standing by himself, and regarding other things as separate. I know an object. How? By its differences from some objects and its likenesses to others; otherwise I could not know it. You cannot think of unity until you have seen variety; you cannot recognise likeness until you have seen unlikeness. The characteristic of intellectual evolution is the discrimination of differences followed by the recognition of likenesses; thus the intellect recognises object after object, each of them by its own characteristic marks. Analysis precedes synthesis. Differences are seen before an underlying unity is recognised.

As this intelligence develops, we find the recognition of the Self and the Not-Self giving rise to struggle all over the world, social struggle as well as mental struggle. In every civilisation in which the intellect is developing from its earlier stages, you must have struggle without in order to stimulate the evolution within; it is a necessary stage, although it be a passing one, and it need not distress us, who see its end, in a world guided by the Gods. All the stages through which a nation passes are necessary for its growth, and need not be condemned merely because of their being limited and imperfect.

In practical politics condemnation is useful as a stimulus, as one of the agents for bringing abou the evolutionary changes, but the philosopher shoul understand, and, understanding, he cannot con demn. The worst struggle that we may see, th most terrible poverty, the most shocking misery, th strife of man against man and nation against natio —all these are working out the Divine purpose and are bringing us towards a richer unity tha without them we could possibly attain.

Let me take one instance which seems to be th most hopeless of all—the instance of war. Wha can be more inhuman than war, what more brut and more terrible, stirring the angriest passions c man and making him like a wild beast in his rage Aye, but that is not all. Let us look at the lif within a soldier which has been evolved by thi terrible discipline without. What is that life learn ing as its vehicles are plunged into strife, into blood shed, into mutilation, into death? It is learnin lessons that without that stern experience it coul not learn, without which its evolution would b checked and be unable to proceed; it is learn ing that there is something greater than th body, something greater than the physical exis ence, something higher, more noble, more com pelling, than the guarding of the physical vehic from injury and even from death; and the poorest soldier who goes out on a campaign, who goes through hardship after hardship, who finds himself frozen with cold or burnt up with heat, who plunges through frozen river or toils across sandy desert, who learns to preserve discipline and submission under hardship, who learns to keep cheerful under difficulty, so that his comrades may not be depressed, who is moved, not by the thought of the body which is suffering, but by the great ideal of the military renown of his regiment, and the safety of the country which he is serving, who is learning thus to sacrifice himself for an ideal, is developing thereby qualities invaluable in lives to come. Need I say this to you, who know the place of the Kshattriya in human evolution? Did Manu when he described these different castes demarcate a caste that had not its place in the evolution of life, that had not something to teach? Was not a man kept in the Kshattriya vehicle until he had learned that life was not dependent on the body, that life was to be held at the service of the ideal, at the service of the mother-land that gave him birth, of the king who ruled him, and who to him stood, as to every Hindu the king should stand, as an Avatâra of God? He learned that when that king called him to the battle-field, he had to give his body to mutilation and to death, because the life that was in him recognised the service of the ideal as evolving the real life, and the body as a mere garment to be thrown aside when duty called? Without that training no Brâhmana could be; no man could come into the caste of the Brâhmana, save as he had gone through that discipline in the ranks of the Kshattriya; because until he had learned that life was everything and form nothing—and that is the lesson which war teaches when it is rightly understood—until that lesson was learned, he was not prepared for the far harder evolution of the life, which is to master the lesson of unity beneath diversity, of love beneath antagonism, of being the friend of every creature and the foe of none.

When the intelligence has developed, when it has reached a fairly high standpoint, the germs of the next aspect of Deity begin to show themselves in man; and that aspect is A'nanda, Joy or Bliss. But in what does A'nanda really consist? It is in the drawing together of separated objects and uniting them into one. That is the essence of Bliss that the very core and heart of the next stage of evolution. In the old days of Hinduism, this was called the life of the Brâhmana, when the Brâhmana was really a Brâhmana and had no further birth before him on the wheel of births and deaths. In the Christian symbology it is called the Christ stage, that of Divine Sonship, and you will find in a great prayer of Jesus, called the Christ, that in praying for His disciples He asked that "they may be one in me,"in union with each other and Himself. There is a grander unity yet, the unity between the Son and Father, a unity of nature not a union of the erst-separated ; but before that unity can be reached, man must have realised the union with his brother men, must see humanity as united, and not as separate; that is, he must have changed his centre of consciousness—that responds to the impacts from without—from the vehicles in which the intellect and the feelings were developed to the life itself,which is one and the same in all. No longer is he to think himself as separate, inasmuch as the "I," the separated self, is now to be transcended, is to be merged in the uniting aspect of the Deity, the Vishnu or the Christ. That is to be developed as the life of man, with all its wonderful beauty and power, with its unifying force. Therefore did Shrî Kṛiṣhṇa come as an Avâtara to this Eastern world to show forth the life of Love; for the life of A'nanda, or Bliss, is ever the life of Love, and by Love alone may we evolve it within ourselves. The aspect of God that is Bliss shows itself as Love; and in word and in action, in simile and in parable, did the

Beloved and the Lover of man reveal that Divine aspect to the longing hearts of his Bhaktas. That was His special work, to show out the Love power of God; and only as that is developed within us can the life take on this lofty unfoldment that knits all selves in the One Self, that sees all lives in Him. Now, in evolution, the Self knows itself as the Life, and is no longer deluded by the ignorance that made it identify itself with the Form; it is life which realises itself as Life. When this stage is reached by the evolving life, the man who was separated becomes Humanity, and is one of the Saviours of the world. There is nothing apart from him, nothing separate to him. He stands in the very Life itself, and sheds his light in every direction into whatever Upâdhi, or vessel, may be in need of it; wherever there is want or cry for his aid, thereto flow his powers. As the sun shines forth in heaven, and may shine unto a million houses, the only condition of his rays entering being that the houses shall lay themselves open to the sunshine, so is the man who has become the second aspect of Deity, in whom that perfection of Divine Sonship is revealed. Man, as the Son of God in Heaven, is above all the distinctions that you find on Earth. He sends down his rays into the waiting hearts of men, and the only condition necessary for his entrance, the one thing that ensures his coming, is that his brother will open his heart to receive him. For he will not break his way in, he will only come where he is welcome. Thus this great life of God shows itself forth now in the man who has become the Saviour, the Son, the Initiate, as a deep compassionate love for all. Every man who reaches that stage is a new force for the uplifting of humanity. Every man who develops that aspect of life is one more wing with which to lift everything upwards. If a man be weak, his life can go to him to strengthen him; if a man be sorrowful, his life can go to him to make him glad; if a man be sinful, his life can go to him to make him pure from sin. To all men he says: "Where-ever a man is there will I meet him, and there will I accept him." That is Shrî Kṛiṣhṇa in manifestation, that the love that shines forth from the bliss aspect of the Human Self.

One step remains, the last, of evolution for this rapidly perfecting life. Again I take up my Christian symbol and venture the quotation:—"As Thou, Father, art in Me and I in Thee, that they also may be one in Us." The Son becomes in fact what he has ever been potentially, one with the Father. He enters into the mighty realm of Self-Being, where God, in the Christian phrase, is "all-in-all." Do not let the narrower presentations of Christianity that here meet you blind you to these fundamental identities of the deeper and more spiritual Christianity with our own ancient faith. Shall these pettinesses, or even outer divergencies, separate those whom the living Spirit would unite? We learn, as we study the Hindu Scriptures, that man after having reached the second stage rises by Yoga, until he attains the last, and becomes one with the Deity Himself in full power of eternal Self-Being. It was because your own Svâmi T. Subba Rao knew this occult truth, which too many know not, that he spoke, as I before mentioned, of the innumerable Centres, or Logoi, in the One, every one of which could be the beginning of a new universe, of a new out-pouring of life. The building of those Centres is a purpose of Life-evolution. The building them up stage by stage is done as the life passes from form to form; and end or ending there is none in the infinite series of the future. What that life holds for us we cannot tell; how should we imagine that far off land, those distant reaches? But this we know: that no will of the Eternal is ever frustrate, no purpose of the Eternal lacks its fruit or misses its goal; and if our eyes fail us in the dazzle of the light wherein we see our unity with the Eternal Father—that unity that transcends our dreaming, when we shall know ourselves to be one with Him—it is enough that at last the evolution of all lives leads into that unimaginable splendour, known only to Íshvara Himself, who pours out His life that we may know it also. And Mahâdeva shall return to It with all the centres that His life has brought into existence, with all the new lives and joys that His imprisonment in His universe has made. That is enough for us to give us the hope—hope, do I say? it is too feeble a word—the joy inexpressible and the certainty which are founded on the very Life of God; for is He not the Truth, the Foundation of the Universe? And when we enter into SAT we shall know the future as we see the past, for we shall be not only immortal but Eternal.

[FOURTH LECTURE.]

EVOLUTION OF FORM.

MY BROTHERS,—We are now to concentrate ou attention on the phenomenal side of the universe that is, on the varied appearances that surround us whether those appearances be visible to the physica eyes or not; for we must remember that the prin ciple of form is to be found in every stage of th manifested universe, and that when the phras "the formless world" is used, the word "formless is only true in relation to the worlds below the on so spoken of. All higher worlds are "formless regarded from below, that is, regarded by the organ of perception which are fitted for exercise in th lower world; but if a person has developed the capa city to respond to the vibrations in any given worl of manifestation, then that world to him is a worl of form and not of formlessness. Everywher manifestation implies form, however subtle may b the matter which composes it; and you may re member that it is said in the *Vishnu Purâna* tha the one characteristic of matter which is alway present is extension, that is, the capacity of taking form, of being shaped in a definite way.

Now before we take up the details of evolution, there are one or two great principles that I want to ask you to keep in mind; for we shall never be able to understand the complexity of detail, if we take it as a series of isolated details; we need to classify these under certain fundamental principles and then, those principles being clear in the mind, we can easily, as it were, pack every detail into its appropriate pigeon-hole in our thought. I shall not trouble you this morning at all with that threefold division of the evolving life with which we dealt yesterday. We can, for our work now, treat life as a unit, speaking of the Divine Life as Íshvara, and of the reflection of that life in man as the Self. We will keep these two terms to avoid confusion: Íshvara as the Divine Life which is the source of evolution; the Self as the human life which is gradually evolving. And we need these two distinguishing names, without going into any of the sub-divisions that we dealt with yesterday in connection with life, in order that we may be able to see how forms are shaped, and to which principle, if I may say so, we are to refer the special modifications.

The next thing that we must realise is the respective functions of these sources of life; one working through the whole kosmos, and therefore coming t man as a part of that kosmos, the other working i man as an individual through the early stages an transcending individuality at the close. The grea life of Íshvara as it rolls outwards, building the universe of forms, expresses itself, as we have seen, b a certain series of vibrations, and every modificatio in the form is the result of an impulse coming b way of vibrations from the ensouling life. Now th point that strikes us most in this manifestation o Íshvara, as we study it, is the unutterable patienc of it. We are impatient for results, He never. W are impatient for results, because, limited by time we crave to see the outcome of our action ; H being the eternal is unspeakably patient, set upo perfection and careless of the time which that perfection may take in evolving. For the evolution o forms this patience is absolutely necessary; whe we come to think, we see that any impatience in th evolution of forms would mean the over-rapi breaking up of the forms. The form is comparatively rigid as compared with the life. If the lif vibrates too rapidly for the form which it is evolving the form will shatter under the stress of those vibrations. Let me give you a very common illustratio to show you what I mean ; a tube of glass, or a ordinary lamp-glass if you like, has a certain not to which it vibrates; and if that note be sung near the lamp-glass, you will hear the note sound out independently from the lamp-glass, as though the lamp-glass were singing; the glass has vibrated in answer to the vibrations of the sound sung to it, it having the capacity of that vibration in it, and thus it reproduces the note. If you increase the force of that note, if you continue vibration after vibration, beyond the point at which the glass is able to respond, your glass will shiver into pieces, shivered by the force of the effort to respond to vibrations beyond its limit of rigidity. I only take that as an illustration, as a picture; it is true in every world of form; and if Íshvara were to send forth vibrations too swift, too subtle for the form which He is ensouling to respond to, that form would be shivered into pieces, and its evolution would be stopped; nature would have again to begin to build a similar form in order to again reach the point which it had already reached. This patience of Íshvara is the thing that strikes us first as we study the evolution of forms. How slow are the changes, how gradual the modifications, what thousands of successive forms are worked in, how wellnigh imperceptible are the changes in their minuteness, although so great when we look at them in the mass; that is one great principle to bear in mind.

Another great principle is the double and parallel action of Íshvara and of the evolving Self. Íshvara is present in the Self of man that is formed within Him. Every evolutionary impulse in the earliest stages comes directly from the life of Íshvara, and as He moulds the form without, He gradually strengthens the centre that He is building up within. His object is to make that centre the image of Himself, self-sustaining; but enormous reaches of time are needed for the building; as He shapes the forms, He builds the centre; and as He builds that centre, and it becomes more and more active, answering to the vibrations that He transmits to it from the outer world, it begins to take on a little action of its own and to send out vibrations, as we may say, on its own account. As this double action goes on within the form, more and more does that evolving centre begin to control the form within which it is developed. As this power of control develops and increases, He withdraws more and more of His directive energy as Íshvara; the energy drawn from Him is now beginning to work *quasi*-independently in the separated centre that He has been building, until at last that centre reflects Himself, and is able to be self-existent by the very life that it has drawn from Him. If this conception be a little abstract, let me give it again in a concrete form. There is one symbol that the sages have used over and over again, in order to express this wonder of the brooding life of Íshvara making an image of Himself and giving to that image the possibility of independent life. It is the symbol of the mother and the child within the womb. As the life of the mother passes into the child that is building within her, transmitting to that new form all the nourishment which is necessary for its growing life, the whole life of the child is dependent on the mother and the life-streams that nourish it are drawn from her own life. The building goes on, and on, and on, till the new centre of life has grown strong, but not until that centre can hold itself together amid the vibrations of the outer universe, is the new form with its ensouling life sent forth on its own independent course. So does the brooding mother-life of Íshvara envelope the children of His love, and so does He nourish them, building them within Himself as the ages pass, until they are able to hold their own centres in the illimitable life of the One, the Supreme. That is another principle which you have to remember throughout the details of the evolution of form.

One other that has two divisions and then the statement of our main principles will be sufficiently complete. There are three aspects, we recollect, which the evolving Self has to unfold. We must add to this a comprehension of the nature of these aspects, when externalised; for we did not yesterday, for lack of time, glance quite precisely at the characteristic outer mark of each aspect of life. As these aspects modify the evolution of form, the form cannot be understood unless its relations to the aspects of life be realised. We have, as we know, to show forth Knowledge, Bliss, and Being. These will come out as powers into the world of form as evolution reaches its later stages, and the form will be able to express those powers of the evolving life. Knowledge, showing forth through form, has as its power Intelligence; Bliss, shown forth through form, has as its power Love; Being shown forth through form, has as its power Existence; so that the fundamental aspects may be said severally to manifest as the powers of intelligence of love, of existence. Otherwise put, the nature o intelligence is knowledge, the nature of love i bliss, the nature of existence is being. The in telligence, love and existence of our worlds are th manifested Knowledge, the manifested Bliss, an the manifested Being of the Self. That is the out ward aspect of the Self as the other is the inne aspect, and these characteristic natures seek thei expression in form. This expression is sought cosmically and individually, alike by the life of Íshvara and the life of the Self. Cosmically they make the planes of the manifested universe, the five planes on which we are evolving. That which manifests as existence, the power of Being, has as its form the Akâsha of the higher realm; that which manifests as love, the power of Bliss, has as its form of matter Vâyu; that which manifests as intelligence, the power of Knowledge, has as its material Agni. These are the three fundamental manifestations in form. The other two are reflections: That which is love, reflecting itself in the lower form of matter —the denser matter of Varuna—takes on the aspect of desire and passion, and becomes kâma. That which is existence, reflecting itself on the yet grosser form of Prithivî, shows forth what we call objective reality. See how the planes correspond, the one with the other. Try and make a picture of a mountain reflected in a lake; and if you have that in your mind, you will follow exactly the way the reflection takes place. There is no reflection of intelligence because it is the central quality; the intelligence is the centre of the five, two are above it and two are below it. It is the central region, the pivot on which the whole has to turn. If you look above to the higher regions, we find love and existence showing themselves forth as the powers of Bliss and Being. That is as it were, the mountain. Now look at your reflection in the lake; the middle part of the mountain is reflected half-way down in the water. The shore is the dividing line between object and image, and represents the intelligence; below that, half-way down, will come the reflection of love showing itself as emotion and desire; then we see the highest peak reflected in the deepest depth of the lake, the existence above, the power of the real Being, reflected below in the plane of physical matter as that illusory existence which man calls real. Try and keep that picture, for the principle of reflection from above to below is one of the keys to understanding both above and below. It helps you to see why emotional love passes into devotion, and how, in the passing from emotion into the higher love which is devotion, it passes from the kâmic plane to the buddhic, where bliss is the distinguishing characteristic; and you will understand why action, the most illusory of things, has to us the sense of reality. It gives that peculiarly definite sense of reality to us because it is the reflection of the real, of the existence of which it is the lower form.

Now these are the principles. Let us try to carry them out in our evolutionary study; for if you hold firm to the principles, the study of detail, of forms, will seem less confusing, less complex and less difficult; you will not lose your way among the trees, when once you have looked down on the forest as a whole; that is a simile I once heard from Professor Huxley, as illustrating principles and details, and it is a suggestive one.

We begin then the detailed evolution of form; it is like a great circle traced downwards and upwards. There is a great difference between the downward arc, the one-half of the circle, and the upward arc, the other half of the circle. In the one case, coming downwards, Íshvara imparts qualities and attributes; in the other half, going upwards, He builds the qualities and attributes into vehicles. These are the two great differences between the downward and upward arcs. In the downward, matter takes up qualities; in the upward, matter is formed into vehicles, or sheaths, or bodies, whatever may be the term we prefer. A process of specialisation goes on, up to a certain point. After a time the specialised materials are drawn together and combined into a vehicle, an organised unity, serving as a tabernacle for the Self. First comes differentiation, and the first step to that is to impart qualities to matter. Let me remind you, as the subject is so difficult a one, what is meant by tattvas, the fundamental forms of matter, and recall once more that passage in the *Vishnu Purâna* where their evolution is described, and where it is stated that the tanmâtra of sound produces A'kâsha; that is, a modification of the consciousness of Íshvara produces the form of matter that we call the atom of A'kâsha; that atom has a mere film of subtlest matter for its envelope, and the vibrating life of Íshvara for the force within. Then we are told that A'kâsha generates another tanmâtra which is touch, and that, enveloped, permeated by A'kâsha, produces the film of denser matter which is called Vâyu, the two tanmâtras and the A'kâsha being the generating force.

This goes on through the whole of the five stages, so that when we get down to the physical plane, we find an atom showing a wall of denser matter, within it the involved life and without it the magnetic field, made up of the higher tanmâtras and their atomic sheaths. The Prithivî atom hence consists of its own tanmâtra plus the matter and the life of Apas; the matter and life of Agni; the matter and life of Vâyu; the matter and life of A'kâsha: so that on the physical plane, the physical atom is a mass of five interpenetrating spheres in which is present as life the whole of the matter and the life of the worlds above it, the envelope, or wall, of the physical atom alone showing forth any characteristics of the physical world—a fact inexpressibly important for evolution. For, each of those sheaths or koshas—as the student of Vedânta calls them, and there is no better word —every one of them is latent in and around the physical atom; and in the upward evolution, every one of them becomes active and strong as evolution proceeds, sheath after sheath being vitalised. How could these koshas, or sheaths, of ours learn to respond to the vibrations of the evolving life, unless every one of them was latently present in us, waiting to be brought into activity? The root of that possibility lies in the atom itself, with all its interpenetrating spheres of life and matter, the sheaths that are within it and around it. That is not the only thing which we understand; as this conception grows clear, we understand a phrase that had often puzzled us in the old days, that "the spirit is senseless on the plane of matter." What does that mean? The spirit, the very essence of consciousness, senseless and helpless on the plane of matter! Why? Because if you take spirit as pure spirit, the intermediate sheaths are not there by which the matter-vibrations are able to reach it, and without these sheaths it is unable to receive and respond to the vibrations of physical matter. It remains unconscious of their very existence, there being no bridge by which they can pass over an affect that life. This is really a perfectly simpl statement of Madame Blavatsky's, but it is one tha I have heard challenged over and over again a entirely meaningless, as conveying no idea, for hov could consciousness be unconscious in any region A little more knowledge would make us less rapi in our condemnation of our betters. That idea then, we will take to help us in the first conceptio of how evolution can take place.

Now let us look how, in the downward arc tha we spoke of, Íshvara is imparting qualities. Accord ing to the nature of the vibrations that He send and of the matter that answers to them will be th quality imparted. As to the idea that differenc of vibrations implies a difference of manifestation let me buttress myself on the great reputation c Sir William Crookes. He issued, two or three year ago, I don't remember the exact date, in 1896 think, a table of vibrations, confined of course t the physical world; a very interesting table, givin a series of classified vibrations and pointing ou which were known to science, and gave rise to wha we call sound, light, electricity, and so on, th difference of vibratory frequency, and the subtlet of the matter in which the vibration was set up giving rise to a particular impression, received an answered by a sensation in us.

That is the principle which I am now applying to our system as a whole. According to the density of the matter will be the rapidity of the vibrations which that matter is capable of expressing; Íshvara sends out vibrations, and the mânasic matter, we will say, is thrown into corresponding vibrations or waves of a frequency identical with those of the life-impulse sent out from Him, so far as it is capable of responding, a limit being set by its fineness on the one side and by its density on the other. Its limit of fineness is the atom of the plane. Its limit of density is the coarsest aggregation of these atoms in the densest solid of the plane. If we take the physical plane for a moment, we have solid, liquid, gas, ether, finer ether, finest ether, and atoms. The lower five are related to the five senses in man as they are at present developed on the physical plane. These five correspond to the sense-organs and the senses that work through them, as is suggested in the names of the tanmâtras. The Solid is related to the sense of Smell; Liquid to the sense of Taste; Fire to the sense of Sight; Air to the sense of Touch; and A'kâsha to the sense of Sound. Now these are not stated in the order given by the western scientist, but I have no time to go into the reason for the difference and to show you where his outer observation fails, because he is not able to trace beyond the limits of his senses into finer working; in dealing with our Vâyu an A'kâsha, he classes them together, and his air i our Agni. These senses and their evolution belon to the upward arc. Coming downwards, Íshvar only gives the power to matter to respond to thes particular vibrations, and these vibrations are cor nected on the physical plane with the sub-division that I have just mentioned, the different sub-div sions of matter, solid, liquid, gas, and so o corresponding in the sense-organs to the senses.

Coming downwards, beginning on the ment plane with Intelligence—missing the two high ones of Existence and Love—He sends out vibra tions to make the matter of the mental plan answer, and the vibrations with which that matte answers, that is, a certain range of vibrations, ar called mental or intelligent. You may say, Why Just for the same reason that in Sir William Crooke tables definite names are given to the differe classes of vibrations, which produce sound, ligh etc., names are given in order to express a certai limit of vibratory force; within one set of limits th vibrations affect the ether, give "light," and th eye receives them. Similarly, vibrations that fa between certain limits of vibratory frequency affe the matter of the third plane, and when they ar received by an organ fitted to focus them in a centre, thus giving rise to self-consciousness, we call that organ Mind, and the action through that Mind, Intelligence. The mere name is as arbitrary as any other name, and we class these under mental, just as a certain range of etheric vibrations is classed as light, is received by an organ fitted to focus them that we call the eye, and the action through that eye is vision. If we are to talk at all, we must have names to describe different classes of phenomena, and we use the word mental or intelligent to describe the range of vibrations working in the particular kind of matter of which, in the upward evolution, an organ is builded that we call the Mind. So, again, to the vibrations that He sends out into the next coarser form of matter, called Apas, or astral, we give the name Sensory. He imparts to them the quality of responding to pleasure and pain, and as He makes this downward sweep He brings into renewed existence on each plane Devas, or beings which have as their characteristic manifestation the quality of their own plane; thus the Devas of the mental plane have the quality of intelligence as their chief peculiarity, and the Devas of the next lower plane have as their chief quality feeling, or the power of sensation, and those of the lowest plane have as their chief quality action, activity. Each Deva class shows out specially tl quality of its plane, and inasmuch as these Dev: draw into their own bodies the matter of the plaı in which they live, they help on its evolution ; f(they draw it in, use it and thus develop it, aı throw it out again into the general reservoir, ju as man draws in physical matter, uses it in his bod and again throws it out into the physical worl As that process goes on and on and on through tl ages, the whole of that kind of matter we ca mental passes through the bodies of these Deva takes on to itself the habit of responding readily the vibrations of intelligence, and thus becom ready for building into the mental body of ma The matter of the astral plane is builded into tl bodies of the Devas of that plane until it takes u this habit of more and more definitely respondir to pleasure and pain, when impacts are made on i and thus can be used for the building up of tl sensory bodies of the lower world. On each plaı this downward sweep brings into activity the: classes of Devas, making the intermediate linl which are to work in the building of forms. Tl essence of the building of forms by a Deva is th: he builds them of the matter of which his ow body is composed. Prepared by that earlier evolı tion, qualities being developed in the downwaı sweep of the life of Íshvara, matter is, in the upward arc, gathered into definite forms, the bodies of plant, animal and man: thus definite vehicles are made, by which the highest consciousness can communicate with, and receive vibrations from, the lowest world.

Let us now, having taken this very rapid sweep downwards, begin to climb upwards. Each kind of matter is now seen to possess certain qualities. Every physical atom has a number of sheaths interpenetrating and surrounding it, the sheath of astral matter with its power of responding to sensation, the sheath of mental matter with its power of responding to intelligence, as well as the sheaths, if they may be called so, of the two higher, Love and Existence, that will not be brought into activity for a long, long time. All is there. Íshvara now begins the great stage of brooding action that I spoke of, the building up of a centre, and it is His first work to build physical forms out of this prepared material, all the Devas of the physical plane being ready to act as His agents, working under His impulse and under the direction of the Lord of the Devas of the physical plane. All these innumerable intermediate agents are wanted; for innumerable are to be the forms, and every one of them has to be builded.

The building of the physical bodies begins wit the formation of the minerals. As a mineral bod is formed, perhaps some crystal, the crystal of a element or a salt, a definite form is built up by Deva of the physical plane. He takes up th material of his own body and such material of th physical plane as is of similar nature to himsel and he begins shaping these crystalline forms. H builds them on the lines of the life-energy sent ot by Íshvara Himself, those lines which Science cal the axes of the crystal, "imaginary" lines; "imag inary"—aye; but they are from the creativ imagination of Íshvara, that is far more potent tha the lower matter in which He builds. That lowe matter follows the creative imagination of the Lorc and these imaginary lines govern the shaping c that crystal that is builded by the Deva. Tyndal believed not in the working of the Devas, ye when he was lecturing on crystals to a popula audience in Manchester he declared that as h pictured to himself the building of a crystal, h found himself imagining tiny architects at work placing every atom with exact precision, with al the intelligence and skill of a human architect, em ployed in making a building. Tyndall was speak ing better than he knew. His imagination wa answering to the truth more keenly than he realisec

For it is the privilege of the man of genius who loves truth as Tyndall did—who was willing to break up every fetter of dogma rather than be a traitor to his conception of truth—to unconsciously intuit the truth that he seeks, so that his words give out a higher meaning than he dreamed of. Tyndall was wise in recommending what he called the scientific flight of the imagination, for that power of imagination is a most useful thing. Never clip the wings of your imagination when you are employed in your scientific work; for it may often give you glimpses of truths that without its aid you would never find. Thus the Devas work and build crystals, and those crystals have some remarkable properties. Professor Japp tells us that some crystals turn a polarised beam of light in a particular way; and he declares that in some of these forms there is a power which is directive and somewhat akin to the intelligence of man. Truly is it akin to human intelligence, inasmuch as it is the parent of human intelligence, the latter being the child that is developing the parental powers. This building goes on through stages on which we must not tarry, through the whole of the mineral world, gradually giving to matter the power to change shape between larger and larger limits without losing cohesion. This is what is called plasticity, the power of changing shape without disintegration. Matter als gains that which science speaks of as elasticity. No what is elasticity? Not, as people generally thinl the mere power of elongation, calling a thing ela: tic that can be pulled out like a piece of Indiá rubber. An elastic body in the popular sens is not an elastic body from the scientific point (view, and, strange as it may sound, glass is muc more elastic than India-rubber. Yet the glass doe not elongate and is brittle. The proper definitio of elasticity is the power of recovering the origin: form after distortion, and matter gradually acquir(this power. As life develops, the equilibrium (the compounds that make up the form becom(more and more unstable, while at the same time tl general cohesion of the form increases; when w come to the higher forms, such as the body of mai we find a power of maintaining the central positic greater than we find in any other form, togeth(with an increased plasticity and elasticity; so that man can adapt himself to the cold of the polar r(gions, and to the heat of the tropics and of the equa torial zone, without losing his body, in a wa that no lower animal can match, that is, he hè the power of adapting his physical body to surrounc ing conditions to a greater extent than is the cas with any other form. Coming back to the miner:

kingdom we left, let us take the next stage; Íshvara can now expand and modify His material a little more than was originally possible without breaking it up. He begins the moulding of the vegetable kingdom, and there also he sets axes of growth, as "imaginary" and as real in their controlling force as in the crystal; though they are not always quite as easy to trace, they are nevertheless there. All the vegetable matter is built in according to these axes, and the natural classification of plants is largely determined by the numerical relations of the parts; thus the law of number shapes the form. As the matter becomes more plastic and yields more readily to the indwelling life, the higher members of that kingdom begin to show the dawning of sensation. That is due to the beginning of the vivification of the next sheath above the physical, composed of what we call astral matter, that which goes to make part of the manomaya kosha of the Vedântin. We see in that a growing susceptibility, an increasing sensory power, very slight in the vegetable world, but still present, and developed much more largely where the vegetable has a long experience of separated life. Take for instance a tree that has endured for centuries, and let me just trace the stages in which the dawning sensation is found, and even a dawn, though I hardly venture to use the word, a dawn of mental quality. That life in tl tree responds to the vibrations received from outsid of cold and heat, of wind and rain, of sunshine ar storm, and as the physical sheath is built up ar developed by the action of the Devas working up(it, the etheric matter in it is continually thrown in vibration by the changes in temperature, light, ai electrical conditions. The vibrations in the ethe that enter into the physical body are passed on the atomic sub-plane, and as the atoms of the phy: cal plane have their spirals made of the coarse matter of the plane of Apas, or astral matter, a slig quivering is caused in that coarsest matter of t astral plane, and that sets up a little movement the tree, responded to by the indwelling life sensation, a massive and general feeling of pleasu or pain.

Have you never walked through a forest, a felt as though all nature were enjoying the sunshir This sensation of pleasure is shown still m(strikingly when the hot season comes to its endir and the first rains fall on the thirsty ground, and t well-nigh withering vegetation sends out a conscic thrill of joy and life renewed. The very trees a bushes rejoice as the rain comes down upon th(with its message of life and of hope. At su moments we recognise that the vegetable world sensitive, although the sensation be widespread, that which is called massive in character.

Forgive me if for a moment I here digress, to say that this fact is one of the reasons why we owe a duty to the vegetable world, not needlessly to cause sensations of dawning suffering. We live too carelessly, my brothers, in this world which is all-living, where there is no atom that is dead, and especially is this sad here in India, where once there was so strong a reverence for life. That is now, alas, beginning to pass away. You are forgetting that all life is Íshvara, that according to the stage of His lower self-evolution is the power of response that is given to the form. In the old days, I remember how, when man took his food, he met the food with gracious greeting because it was sacrificing its life in order to build, through that sacrifice, his own. Though it did not possess the higher powers of sensation as we find them in the animal, but only the lesser sensation powers of the vegetable world, still, even then, he met it with reverence, as a sacrifice which was being made to him, and took it with gratitude and with love; that lower life was yielding itself up to him for his upbuilding. But to-day, so lost is that gentle grace in many of our Hindu people, that they not only disregard the sacrificed lives of the vegetable kingdom but also those of the far more sentient forms whi(Íshvara has developed in the animal kingdom of H world. We find men who wear the outer shape the Hindu, who have his colour, his form, his fac who boast themselves of their descent from antiquit who hold themselves therefore in thought above tl western nations, forgetting the life of the Self this sentient creation, and nourishing their bodi with the bodies of their lower brethren, witho showing any sense of the sacrifice made, or feeli even a passing gratitude for the life which is giv for them.

Let us come back to the tracing of our form Íshvara, brooding over the evolving forms, co tinues His patient work—patient, that the form m never be broken by an overstrain, but may be slow developed into a vehicle of the life that ensouls In every form He lives, evolving it, but He lim with illimitable patience His manifestation of li to the poor capacities of the form, that it may gr and not be destroyed. Do you remember an c story of the ancient days, in which most of y would be ashamed to acknowledge belief, for a you not graduates and men of western knowledg Though descendants from the old time, you ha naught to do with it, but I, who was trained in t West, I have no feeling of shame in acknowledgi my belief in the strange things that come down to us from the times when truth was less veiled than it is now. So I dare to recall the story to you, although you may think that it is but a fable or legend. There was a boy who believed in Vishnu or Hari, in whom his father believed not, Prahlâda he was named; and that boy went through many trials, but in all his faith in the Supreme defended him; at last his father, scoffing, said, turning to a pillar in his room: "You tell me that Hari is everywhere: is He in that pillar?" "O Hari, Hari!" cried the boy, and forth from the pillar in the form of a Lion burst an avatâra of Vishnu and the pillar was shivered into pieces. Truly is He everywhere, in every particle of matter; there is no one particle from which He cannot come forth in all the might of His Godhood, in all the majesty of His Deity. But He will not, because if He did, the form could not bear that revealing, and would shiver into pieces as the God appeared. A profound truth, even if you regard the story as an allegory, a truth which teaches us what evolution means.

Thus Íshvara worked on age after age and æon after æon, with that marvellous patience of which I spoke, until matter was made sufficiently plastic to build it into the form in which His highest life was to begin its development, the form of man; building that form, He begins also to strengthen very mucl the centre which the form is for a while to protect Let me say in passing one thing that I have omitted that whenever a form has reached its highest possi ble point, its limit of expansion, He breaks it, in orde that, in a new form better adapted, the ensoulin life may continue to grow; for He knows when t break as well as when to hold; He knows whe to destroy as well as when to preserve; and th moment that the limit of a form has been reachec and its matter can yield no further, He bursts th form asunder, that its materials may recombin themselves, under the impulse of life, into a mor plastic organism, and that the life may thus gai further evolution, ensouling a higher form mor fitted for the expression of its increasing power We call this breaking of the form death, and w fear and shrink from it, and if people talk to us c death, in the flush of our life, it comes as a jar an a shock. But, as I told you in the beginning, yo may see very plainly that death is that beneficen aspect of Íshvara, which breaks a form that ha become a prison, in order to give the life a new forr in which it may continue to grow; He breaks th rigid form when it can develop no further, an gives the life the plastic form of a baby, that ma be shaped more easily by the moulding forces c the life within it, yielding itself to every impulse from within. It seems then, that when we see things rightly, we should hail death as birth rather than as death. For looked at from the side of life, every death is a being born into the higher possibilities of a new shape that will adapt itself to the growing life.

When man begins his long pilgrimage, a form is ready for his ensouling, prepared to receive and to respond to the impulses which come to it from the physical, astral and—to a small extent—from the mental planes. His physical atoms are considerably evolved, the sensory sheath is working actively, and there is a very imperfect lower mental sheath; these have been built up through the evolution of the animal realm. Do not fall into the mistake of the western way of thinking, and say that man descends from the animal; that is not true. It is only a fragment of truth half seen and thereby distorted. What is true is this: that the matter of his lower vehicles has been prepared by evolving through the stages of the elemental, mineral, vegetable and animal kingdoms, in order that it may be builded into the form of man; that *in previous kalpas* forms had been evolved that might fairly be described as half-ape, half-human, that were never occupied by the triple Self, and that therefore belonged to the animal, not to the human kingdom; that in the present cycle the human form evolved, as a fœtus evolves, passing rapidly through the lower stages on the way to the human, as in pre-natal life, and it therefore has stamped upon it the stages through which it has passed. I have been going over, roughly and swiftly, those stages through which the matter of which the body is composed has gone in the past, and you will see that the true theory of evolution is different from the somewhat crude view that there is a regular succession of births from the animal into the man. The matter has been made plastic in the animal, but man in his form is the result of a higher working; the germ of his life can never develop into the animal, but only into the human, because more has been infolded into it, and that germ must unfold along a line which is that of direct human growth. Remembering that, to prevent a possible misconception, we turn to the human centre that is now definitely formed. We speak of its encircling form as the causal body, or Karana Sharîra, the form by which the Self is limited; the Karana Sharîra is not the Self, remember, but is the containing vehicle of the triple Self, and the organ of one aspect of that Self, the aspect of knowledge, shown forth as intelligence. This sheath is important, being relatively of a permanent nature, and it goes on from birth to birth; death cannot touch it, birth cannot modify it; it is the treasure-house or receptacle of all the qualities acquired by experience through human evolution, and passes through the whole cycle of re-incarnations; it is the special *human* characteristic. The form begins to adapt itself more and more to the life, and here comes in a growing difficulty. The characteristic of the life of man is the life of the intellect; this the specifically human part of evolution; but the life of sensation is far more vivid and tumultuous in the beginning, and the earlier stages of form are adapted to answer to these impulses. You may ask, why not give the man at once a mental body only, in which to work out his evolution, why must he struggle through the evolution of this body of sensation? Because, if he misses that stage, he will not be able to make up the links which are necessary for the continuity of his consciousness. At a later time the perfect man is conscious on all planes from Nirvâna downward to the physical, from the physical upwards to Nirvâna. On every plane in unbroken continuity of consciousness the Jîvanmukta lives and works. There is no link lacking. If, then, the man does not establish, in the building of his body of sensation, certain centres or, as they are called, chakras—that drawing into centres which is the work of the upward arc, as giving qualities is the work of the downward arc—if he does not draw the powers of sensation into definite centres in the sheath of his astral body, he will not have the links which he requires to receive impacts from the astral plane, and through which he can send out thrills of consciousness in order to impress it, rule it and guide it. That is why there is so much delay in the savage condition, where the life of sensation is supreme; these astral chakras are being builded up as centres of the senses, and they are built firm and strong; the outer organs, the eye, the ear, the nose, the tongue, the skin, these are merely the necessary organs in the physical body for the expression of consciousness through these chakras.

If we take, for a moment, a swift survey of the evolution of forms, we shall find that the building of organs follows the exercise of life-functions; in the earliest forms there are no organs, but the functions of life are present and active; the creature breathes and assimilates, circulation goes on; but there are no organs for digestion, no organs for breathing, no organs for circulation; the whole body does everything. But as evolution proceeds and definite organs are formed in the physical body, in the nervous system, and as later, in the astral body, chakras or astral centres of sensation are formed—as this goes on, we find a more specialised being developed with definite organs. Always the organ comes after the function, and through the organ the function expresses itself more and more perfectly. That is a fundamental principle. And do not forget that in this you are on what is thought the safer ground of western science. You do not find an organ appearing before the development of its function. You always find the life-impulse first, and then the moulding of the matter into a shape which enables that impulse to express itself more perfectly. If we trace evolution from the amœba upwards we find differentiation and specialisation becoming more marked the whole way through, yet man himself turns round, and with the very brain which has been formed under the vibrations of intelligence he reverses the whole process, and asserts that thought is produced by the brain; but every organ is formed as the organ of a function, it is produced by life, and is not its creator.

This process goes on until the necessary organs are made and the nervous system is linked to the chakras in the astral body, chiefly through what is called the sympathetic system. There are certain nervous cells of a peculiar kind in that system, of which modern science does not say much, beyond giving you the forms and contents, and these are the links between consciousness in the physical body and in the sensory body. Then come the chakras already spoken of as the centres for the working of consciousness in the astral body. A similar process goes on in the mental body under the action of thought-impulses, and there we have also an organised body able to respond to different kinds of thought, and thus to serve consciousness as its organ for expression in the mental world. As we grow mentally we build our organs for consciousness.

Coming to this building of form practically, we learn that we organise the body of sensation to higher purposes by checking the life-impulse as it runs out to the object of the senses. These objects gradually turn away from the abstemious dweller in the body, it is written, and as the lower world ceases to attract, the higher world begins to use the form for nobler ends. If we desire to increase mental power, we must practise steady thinking, and check the rovings of intelligence over the phenomenal world. As a matter of fact, many people never really think at all; what they call their thoughts are nothing more than the reflections of other people's thoughts to which their consciousness responds; their minds are looking-glasses, not productive organisms; most men's minds, I fear, are looking-glasses reflecting objects that are before them, and contemplating these reflections a man says to himself: "See! how I am thinking!" when he is only repeating the thoughts of others. Now we are not to be mere looking-glasses; when the objects of the outer world give rise to images, the mind is to work on them, analyse, re-arrange, combine; thinking is the work of the mind itself on the mental images supplied through sensation, the working on the materials which have been gradually gathered by experience. As soon might you call a loose heap of bricks that you see in the compound of a house, a building, as call the reflection of other people's thoughts, your thinking. That is only the material for thought. Thinking is the work of the architect, of the builder that builds these bricks into a definite edifice, and until we have built up thoughts in our minds, we have no right to arrogate to ourselves the name of thinkers. Practise then this independent thinking; it is hard; you will not know how hard until you try it. Never let pass a day without reading something that gives you material for thought. No matter if the book be not religious; if it be only intellectual, that will make you stronger in intellect. Even leaving spirituality aside with its nobler possibilities, take some great book worthy of being thought over, not a newspaper, not a sensational novel, not a child's book, but a BOOK—an original book, on a real topic; what Charles Lamb called a book. Read, but do not read much, perhaps not more than a dozen or twenty lines; think these lines over and over and over for at least thrice as long as you have taken to read them slowly. Do that every day regularly, and do not miss it. You find time for your dinner; why, if you can find time to feed your body and to talk, can you not find time to feed your mind? Then your mind would grow. If you do that as an experiment, say for three months only, never missing a day—for if you miss a day, you will slip back and lose the value of the automatic action of your mind—do that for three months as an experiment, as a scientific man makes an experiment, and thus train yourselves for three months in power of close attention and thought, and at the end of the three months, you will be startled to find how much these powers have grown. When you have put yourself through this experiment, then you will not want a lecturer to tell you about the value of such self-discipline, for you yourself will have proved it to be good. Take one faculty after another to train; train your reasoning faculty, your memory, your power of comparison and contrast. Take up a faculty, just as any one takes up a study that he is working at, and work at it until you are an artist in that particular faculty.

That is how form is builded, when the human Self is beginning to co-operate with the work of Íshvara, when the centre is beginning to take the control of its vehicles. It rationalises its workings, and builds and modifies them step by step. When this has been done for many lives, then comes the life for Yoga; then the man may be taught how to make more rapid progress, and how to vivify the inner and subtler sheaths of his being by certain practices, that will be taught him the moment he is ready—but that will never be taught him until he *is* ready, nay though he range the world over in search of a Guru, or live the life of an ascetic in the cave or in the jungle. That is not enough, so long as his desire is unconquered, so long as his mind is still restless. When the senses are dominated, when the mind is controlled, and not before—but then, as certainly as before there will not be the coming—a Guru will appear who will take that man by the hand and lead him along the path that is narrow as the edge of a razor, that may only be trodden by the controlled in sense and by the steady in mind, for the fall either to the one side or to the other means delay for many a birth to come. Then is developed that aspect of Bliss which shows itself outwardly as love; a faint reflection of that bliss is felt in many stages of meditation, and joy has birth within you, wells up within you, enwraps you fold by fold, until you in yogic trance reach the true A'nanda, which is the essence of beauty, and makes you quiver under its subtle vibrations of ineffable delight. And later, later still, at a stage that you may reach, when all is purified through long evolution, there comes the rising into the highest, where the subtlest matter becomes the vehicle of that developed centre, now no longer a circumference restraining and necessary, but an obedient vehicle which will serve when it is wanted and fall away when wanted it is not. As it is written that in the A'kâsha there is every possibility of form, so the life that has reached Self-existence is a being that garbs itself in any form by gathering the A'kâsha around it. Thus it may develop vehicle after vehicle until the whole of the human series is builded for use, but none of them is prison for limitation; then we say that the man is a Jîvanmukta, He is free, and all matter has become His servant, to use when He has need of it, to cast aside when He needs it not; every region of the world is His to use, no region of the world is its own to bind Him; He is liberated, and as the liberated Self He may, if He will, still work for His brother men, remaining, as Shrî Shankarâchârya taught us, until the end of His age, in order to lift humanity more rapidly on its upward climb. Thus are formed Those who are the co-workers of Íshvara in the helping of humanity, who, having gone through all suffering, throw everything they have gained at the feet of the Lord, who turn back to the world, never again to be bound by it, but still responding to the compassion which is the very life of Íshvara Himself. As long as Íshvara wills to remain in manifestation, so long does He whose will is one with that of Íshvara, will also to remain. He has nothing to gain, nothing to learn, nothing to take that any world can give Him; but He stands beside His Lord as an organ of the expression of the highest life, existing no longer for anything that He takes, but as the channel of the life of God. That is the prize of our calling, that the goal on which our hearts are fixed.